REVIEWS REVIEWED

Can a book written for teenage eyes be worth reading if parents, much less chers (even probation officers) ...ou decide...

THANKS

"It's so simple, even olde... ..get a lot out of it." *Ann, 16, Jacksonville, ...ida*

"*It's the best book I ever read in my entire life.*" Miriam, 16, Atlantic Beach, New York

"It helped me understand myself and my friends better." *Sue, 15, Glendale, California*

"*I used it for a book report and got my first A+.*" Scott, 17, Calistoga, California

"The waters are still rough, but now I've learned to sail with the current without worrying about every wave." *Keisita, 18, Kjaerarsvej, Denmark*

"*For the first time I understand my parents.*" Freida, 15, Sedona, Arizona

"Guess what — I got kicked out of Algebra for reading your book!" *Thad, 17, Farmington, New Mexico*

"When I first got hold of the book I didn't want to read it — my mom gave it to me. Six months later when I had nothing to do, I took a look at it. Amazingly it made sense ..." Nancy, 15, Van Nuys, California.

"I really felt impressed with your book. I still read it every day like my life depends on it." *Scott, 16, Chicago, Illinois*

"It taught me things I wasn't taught." Phil, 17, Austin, Texas

"That book opened a lot of windows and taught me how to gain self-confidence." *Wes, 15, Fullerton, California*

"What's written is so logical and practical ..." Frank, 18, Pensacola, Florida

"Parents should be made to read this." *Sylvia, 15, Lexington, Kentucky*

"It tells me what I'm going through to a 'T.' It's good to know I'm not the only one with these problems." Kevin, 17, Salt Lake City, Utah

"The book channels energies in the right direction. I just wish it could reach everyone." *Annie, 15, Long Beach, California*

"It helped us cope with several crises." Mr. & Mrs. E.L., Ann Arbor, Michigan

"Please send 6 copies—we want to share the book with other families." H.L. MD, Denver, Colorado

"I walked into my daughter's room late last night thinking she was sneaking tube time, and found her locked into your book. That's never happened before." B.P., Palo Alto, California

TESTIMONIALS FROM TEACHERS

"By far the best book written for teenagers…"
Mrs. L.R., San Marcos, California

"This book should be part of every high school curriculum in the U.S." Ms. L.A.M, Yonkers, New York

"I want to purchase a copy for every student in my Alternate program." H.H., Palos Verde, California

"After considerable agonizing with our principal and PTA, I received permission to use the manual in my Senior Problems classes. The kids are wild about it." Ms. P.P., St. Louis, Missouri

"Why don't you get our school district to put this book in the libraries?" Mr. J.L., Chicago, Illinois

PRAISE FROM PARENTS

"The manual did what two college degrees, 15 years of professional experience, a couple of marriages and 38 years of living failed to accomplish." *Mrs. S.W., San Antonio, Texas*

"*I wish to heaven I had something like this 40 years ago.*" Mr. G.J., San Francisco, California

"There's so much love in this house since we read the book." *Mrs. S.C jr, Memphis, Tennessee*

"*After our 16-year old left home, she got a copy of Teenage Survival Manual and now she's back. It's a whole new beginning. Thank you, thank you, thank you.*" Mrs. G.W., Nevada City, California

"I woke up and found my husband finishing your manual, at 3 A.M. He wants to order 12 copies…" *E.H., Key West, Florida*

"*I had forgotten how it was to be 16 when nobody trusts you. (The book) really helped me be with my kids.*" Mrs. S.S., Monterey, California

"You don't treat teenagers like a disease only time will cure." *Mrs. S.W.C., Sacramento, California*

"…with only 6 copies to go around, the students actually fight over who gets to take one home." *Mrs. K.H., W. Los Angeles, California*

PLAUDITS FROM OTHER PROFESSIONALS

"Keep writing. You have the pulse on the teenage phenomenon." *L.F. United Methodist Church, Washington*

"We've been using the manual with great success for rap sessions with counselors, mental health workers, teachers and teens. " JLR, M.S.W. (A Southwest Counseling Service)

"This looks to be a special book that would help me 'see' what some of my kids are going through." *KJH, L.L.D., Juvenile Div., Ninth Judicial District Court, Douglas Co., Nevada*

"Many teachers, church groups, parent counseling classes in the lodge find this book answers their needs so well." V.P., Workshop Director, CA

"Your book is required reading before granting probation." *D.T.B., MSW, Delaware County Juvenile Detention Center, Pennsylvania*

"For several years now, our chapters have used your book to nurture young people's spiritual education, leadership skills and a sense of who and what they are..." T.P., Coordinator, International Youth of Unity (Y.O.U.), Missouri

"...it helps the kids survive Alaska's long winters." L.H., Norton Sound Health Corp.

RAVES FROM REVIEWERS

"Unlike others, the book is written for adolescents; parents will learn a lot from the advice, too." MIDWEST BOOK REVIEW

"I was skeptical... thought it would be loose and compromising but was pleasantly, gratefully surprised. It's an important book—clear, passionate." Guru R.K.K., Sikh Youth Federation of Canada

"I can't tell you how impressed I am with your approach. I'll crib big chunks for my show." P.H., Talk Show Host, California

"This is one of the only books of its genre that affords teens the respect that they can regard serious subjects seriously. It does not mince words and there is no 'mall talk.' This should be the text for a required course in life offered to junior and senior high school students." NAPRA Review.

TEENAGE SURVIVAL MANUAL

How to Reach 20 in One Piece
(And Enjoy Every Step of the Journey)

NEW MILLENNIUM EDITION
BY
H. SAMM COOMBS

HALO BOOKS
San Francisco

Library of Congress Cataloging-in-Publication Data

Coombs, H. Samm, 1928
  Teenage survival manual : how to reach 20 in one piece (and enjoy
every step of the journey) / by H. Samm Coombs. — New millennium ed., 5th ed.
    p. cm.
  Summary: A guide for teenagers seeking self-confidence,
independence, social values, a spiritual grounding, a vision for the
future, and the responsibilities this involves.
    ISBN 1-879904-18-7
  1. Teenagers--Conduct of life. 2. Self-realization--Juvenile literature.
S. New Age movement--Juvenile literature. of   [1. Conduct of 1ife.]
I. Title.
BJ1661.C64 1998
248.8'3--dc21   97-21273
                                                              CIP
                                                               AC

TEENAGE SURVIVAL MANUAL

Published by Halo Books, Inc.

P.O. Box 2529, San Francisco, CA 94126

Printed in the United States of America

First Edition published 1977
Second Edition published 1978
Reprinted 1979
Third Edition published 1981
Reprinted 1983, 1985, 1988
Fourth Edition published 1989.
Reprinted 1991, 1993
Revised 1995
Fifth Edition published 1998
Current edition's most recent printing indicated by first digit below:
2   3   4   5   6   7   8   9   10

ISBN 1-879904-18-7

DEDICATION

To my helpmate, Shirley Coombs,
and Tom Perine, Tom James, Jerry Fogelson,
Hedda Lark, Mrs. Elvidge, Mr. Littlejohn, sages
past & present, and especially my mother.

ACKNOWLEDGEMENTS

Thank you Dick Moore and Stephanie Lipney for
your illustrations; Scott Coombs for your proof-
reading and editorial assistance, Diane Spencer
Hume for your technical assistance, Jefferson
Coombs for your Devil's Advocacy; Librarians
and booksellers for the spaces in your places.

One ship drives east,
and another drives west
With the selfsame
winds that blow,
'Tis the set of the sails
and not the gales
Which tells us the way to go.

Winds of Fate
Ella Wheeler Wilcox

TABLE OF CONTENTS

AUTHOR'S PREFACE

Based on the mail I receive, a lot of parents, teachers and all kinds of other non-teenagers find this book of interest. But it's not written for them.

Because it's intended for teenage eyes, I'm only interested in *your* concerns and questions. And I am pretty sure you are questioning if anyone past '30' can deal with your concerns in a meaningful way. The proof of the pudding, as they say, is in the eating. A few bites will tell you if it's going to be just a lot of fluff or something tasty and nourishing.

You might also ask, "What motivates a grown-up to write a book about growing up?"

No voice in the night commanded me. I have no guru to impress, no church to fill or cult to cultivate. But I did have a son approaching his teens when this was first written. Like most fathers, I felt called on to raise a torch to help him steer clear of the pitfalls I have met along life's path, as well as previewing some of the pleasures to be enjoyed en route.

Also involved is a conviction that human history might stop repeating itself if just one generation were to grow up conscious of its power and responsibilities. Once aware of your potential, you may choose to shed the acts and armor inherited from the past without feeling threatened.

I do not mean to suggest this book will usher in the Aquarian Age. But it's a step in the right direction, aimed as it is at the people who will fly Spaceship Earth through the next century. A teenager is a lot closer to making his/her life work than are most adults—closer by virtue of not having had time to go too far astray. The beginning is a very good place to get started on the right foot.

—H. Samm Coombs
Black Point, California

FIRSTWORD

Congratulations!

By opening this book you've shut a lot of mouths that have been telling the world it's impossible to communicate with teenagers unless the message is carried on primetime TV or buried in the lyric of a Top 40 tune.

Of course, opening a book is not finishing it. But, "a journey of a thousand miles begins with the first step," which you have just taken! Now proceed at whatever speed suits your mood. There's no rush—this isn't some kind of assignment. You might want to place your "manual" next to your bed and chew on a chapter before ZZZzzzing. Ideas are more digestible when you're horizontal. And the alpha waves your brain generates on the threshold of sleep have a way of making invisible things like ideas meaningful and useful.

You'll come across more than a few words that are new to you. Unlike too many books addressed to young people, this one isn't going to stoop to conquer—instead of speaking in the private lingo popular at this moment in time, this book employs language that will be operative when it comes time to hand the book to your kids. Anyway, how're you going to expand your vocabulary and stretch your mind if you don't ever confront something new? In most cases you won't even have to look up the words as they'll be surrounded with contextual words you're familiar with. "Contextual" being a case in point!

While this is a "How-To" manual, it's not a *work-book*. The object of these paragraphs is to help you ENJOY this life to the fullest. There is no higher or better use of human existence. For when joy is lacking, so is compassion, pride, freedom. Nothing will satisfy a person incapable of enJOYment. And joyless people are inclined to interfere with their neighbors' joys.

No skipping

The first part of this book is stacked with stuff that makes what follows lots more meaningful. So don't go rushing ahead to the "S-E-X" chapter until you've opened your mind to the previous bits on "Responsibility" and "Opposites" and "The Two Realities," etcetera. Like the song says, "...the very beginning is a very good place to start." That way you at least know when you've reached The End.

Additional Editions

The First Edition of this book was sponsored by The Centers For Teenage Discovery as a review of experiences that came up in the Center's self-discovery workshops. But it soon became apparent the book should have a life of its own as it would touch more lives and serve more people than ever the workshops could (they being limited by time, place, and money). So a Second Edition was published for national distribution … followed by subsequent editions (including foreign language editions) and numerous reprintings to address matters of the moment: AIDS, the Kamikaze behavior of contemporary teens, melting polar ice caps, designer drugs and other exciting, real-world stuff.

Word Play

The success this book has enjoyed to-date should tell the publisher to "leave well enough alone … don't fix what works!" Good advice, but it is only human to wish to improve on the past. Words are weird devices—they mean different things at different times to different people. Words are like a blob of damp modeling clay—so full of possibilities; so hard to keep hands-off. Especially when those words deal with the Art of Living: how to keep your head screwed-on right.

Making a bookful of words appealing and meaningful to you is no easy task. It's not a question of intelligence (you've got enough of that to keep the author on his toes). It's a matter of interest. Keeping a 16-year old interested in the printed word requires some pretty zingy stuff. It also means resisting the temptation to write what the P.T.A., the F.B.I., the Board of Education, and U-2 think is appropriate. You get plenty of that already!

Why?

It is fair to ask why this modest manual has been cheered by teenagers, saluted by parents, applauded by educators and other concerned professionals. What's in it that isn't to be found in other books about the greening years?

Well, the first thing to know is that blessed few books about the teen years are written *for* teens! Apparently, publishers subscribe to the conventional wisdom that teenagers can't or won't read what some adult has to say about their experience.

The second thing to know is what little there is to read about the threshold years concentrates on the world of form and function without acknowledging the inner realms of being and feeling. Here again is the adult assumption that teenagers wouldn't be interested in worlds of their own making. Com'on folks, where were you when the flower children planted diamonds in the sky (whose blossoms we're still gathering)?

1

SEVEN YEARS
OF HEAVEN
AND HELL

You are at the point where
any future can overtake you

The library is packed with learned books about every stage of growing up. And each phase is said to be critical, some kind of crisis or Moment of Truth.

Well, there are moments, and there are *moments!* The present moment is probably as momentous as any you'll experience; at least until you reach the flipside of the teenage years, the frantic fifties, when your body starts folding instead of unfolding.

So it's not just your imagination—a lot of stuff is happening to you these daze that has never happened before, and will never happen again. For some of you it's confusing, frustrating, maybe emotionally painful. For others it's just great, a super good time. One thing the teen years are *not*, not for anyone, are boring.

3

Luck has nothing to do with it

The fact that the teenage period is an upper for some and a double downer for others serves to introduce one of life's great mysteries. How come? Why does everything good seem to happen to some people while a black cloud shadows others? One thing's for sure—it has nothing to do with luck. It is impossible to isolate any single cause of one person's downfall or another's success—why Joan's a genius and Dick's a dummy, or why Tom survived the ghetto while Sally became a teenage prostitute. A person(ality) is an evolving ecological system (that affects the whole Universe and is, in turn, affected by it).

"Every minute you are a full statement of your being." That is to say—you are always the sum total of your past up to the present. Every one of your actions to-date, every thought, every mouthful of food, every secret desire, each and every word you utter adds up to the person you are at this moment in time. So there's no denying your past; no way to wipe it out. But that's no reason to walk backwards through life focused on what has happened. The way to avoid pitfalls and surmount hurdles is to face them.

Many believe the past is not just the remembered past but includes past incarnations; past lives if you prefer. You did not spring out of nothingness. It's bad logic as well as bad physics to think nothing can become something. (Neither can something become nothing!)

The ingenious gene

Your consciousness has stored every impression since it became conscious. This memory bank generates certain inclinations or tendencies, attitudes and aptitudes. You tend to be a certain kind of person. Also contributing to your tendencies is environment: the sum total of social, economic, educational, political, cultural, even climatic conditions surrounding your life to-date. And then there is heredity. The ingenious gene arranges the physical facts of your life.

To complicate the mixture even more: certain kind of faces and physiques lead to certain kind of experiences that influence your mind/consciousness. This is the field of 'Behavioral Genetics.' Why, for-example, are people with skinny, fragile physiques so often nervous, shy individuals? Probably because skinny, fragile kids get pushed around a lot. Appearance does seem to shape experience that shapes character.

Making the most of what-is

It is worthless to wonder which of these parts of your past has the most impact on your present. What is, *is!* The only question to ask is: what are you doing with what-is?

The past is powerful, but you are not its pawn. You are not powerless over it. That energizing force called willpower is capable to rising above or transcending the past.

Excuses, excuses...

To say 'bad blood' or a bad neighborhood determines the outcome of one's life is a cop-out. You can make your life come out any way you wish. While some of us must overcome more disadvantages than others; it can be done. The higher the wall separating you from your objectives, the stronger you'll be after surmounting it. Every disadvantage produces an advantage. Of course people don't want to know this. Most people only want excuses.

We love to consider ourselves victims of forces beyond our control. Hogwash. This doesn't mean various people don't have real limitations. But those handicaps have more to do with your physical package than the 'real' you: the inspector; that immaterial part of you that witnesses the physical world. So a one-legged person would be foolish to wish to become an Olympic high-hurdler, and wise to concentrate on chess or computer programming. But that is not really the point of this chapter.

Soloing

While it's never too early and never too late to get your act together, a person just doesn't have all the necessary equipment or the motivation before 14 or 15. As a general rule, your body is going through such dramatic changes prior to 14 that it is asking too much of an adolescent to do anything more than keep two feet on the ground. Changing from a caterpillar to a butterfly is quite enough without expecting he/she to understand what's going on. 12 to 14 is a hanging-in-there period. But come 15, you're ready to fly; physically ready. The fact that so many of you suffer broken wings in the process indicates there's more to flying than equipment. There's overcoming fear; developing confidence and technique. But that's still not the point of this chapter.

Fasten seat belts

The point is this: Between 15 and 18 comes the first opportunity to decide how you want your life to be. At 15 you've got the body and the basic smarts to get your act together. There's no equivalent to these three momentous years. People are 'young adults' for a good ten years (depending on who's doing the counting). And you'll be an adult for some twenty years. And an old adult for another thirty-plus years. 15 to 18 is just a tick of time compared to those upcoming periods. And yet within these brief teenage years, such a lot of new stuff comes down on you: sex, higher education, financial independence, career choices, lifestyle options, legal responsibilities, maybe even love.

15 to 18 is a crash course in lifemanship. Think of all the new sensations, realizations, experiences that

occur in that short span. (Adults have been known to go for decades without coming up against anything new!) And for the first time you'll face the full force of society's prohibitions (all the 'do nots') and expectations (all the 'dos'). How about that—just when you're ready to soar, life comes along and burdens you with all that baggage. That's life. What a downer. Doesn't seem fair, does it? Well it is—as you will see in an upcoming chapter.

The long and the short of it

Because the teen years are such a brief encounter —however long and drawn-out they may seem to you—the adult world is inclined to look the other way. That's one reason teenagers are so isolated: why there's so little literature written *for* teenagers (and none written *by* teenagers); why so few organizations exist to represent you; why teenagers have no clout, no authority, no 'rights.' There's just no time to get organized. The 16 year-old who decides to become an advocate for teenage 'rights' will be 21 before anyone listens. Then he/she is no longer interested.

But for all the apparent problems that are unique to these three or four tumultuous years, there are some unique advantages—golden opportunities which will never again occur. Number one among these is the opportunity to be your self.

Notes to My Self

2

GETTING YOUR ACT TOGETHER

Don't laugh at a youth for his affectations;
he's only trying on one face after another
till he finds his own.
—Logan Pearsall Smith

Be yourself." When someone says that, they usually mean, "Stop acting, quit pretending ... be real." Being 'real' should be the easiest of all things to be. You shouldn't have to work at being 'real.' You shouldn't have to study how to be 'real,' or spend time in front of a mirror deciding who the 'real' you is. And yet, most of us have a difficult time being what we in fact are. That goes for adults as well as teenagers. You are so busy being a student, a football star, a lover, a trouble-maker or a Tomboy that you're left with no time or place to be whatever it is that's behind those masks.

Jails without walls
Very early in life we are handed scripts and are expected to act accordingly. We go through all these

acts without ever getting in touch with who's doing the acting. That's a trap; a jail without walls. Most people remain prisoners to their own acts without knowing how easy (and essential) it is to be free.

It is impossible for a doctor to develop any self-confidence if he thinks he's simply a doctor. He may be confident of his doctoring abilities, but that's not *self*- confidence. There's nothing wrong with being a doctor or a piano player or a homemaker or a Congressman. That's what bodies and brains do. But you are more than a body and a brain. If you don't think so, why do you call it *your* body, *your* brain? How come you can lose a finger or all four limbs and still be you?

What is critically important is that you realize the difference between you and the roles you play. What a difference that makes. It provides you with an anchor to hold you steady in stormy times. You'll never need to sing that sad song, "Is That All There Is?" When you know that your roles are not you; that they are just what the external you (the ego!) is currently doing —what goeswith you— then you can handle the ups and downs that come with playing doctor, housewife, singer, burglar, lover, President or teenager. That allows your consciousness to watch and witness what is happening to your physical parts and ego.

Taking charge

When you can separate your self from your roles, then you are both the Actor and the Director. That puts you in complete charge of the whole production. You can continue to play your role(s) better able to accept what happens to the character you're playing. If things get too heavy, you The Director can step in and change the scenery, the script, the interpretation. Try it. It's easy.

When you wake up with a face full of zits (making difficult your role as the most-beautiful-girl-in-the-sophomore-class), realize that what is happening to your face is zits. You are not zits. Your face has them. That doesn't make them go away. If pimples are a problem, you've got a problem! If all you are is a Beautiful Girl, then you are no more! Sorry. Your life is ruined. But if you can witness/observe you having this problem and say, "Oh, dear—what's happening to me right now is a lousy complexion," then you've separated your consciousness from what's happening to your face. That places you in the driver's seat. You are no longer a victim, being taken for a ride by forces beyond your control.

The roles we play

Of course most people—whether 15 or 50—think they know who they are. They'll recite a list of titles or attributes—goeswith things like, "I am a man; a tall dark and handsome fellow who's an architect; a Republican, and a Methodist." They also will tell you what they want to be: a millionaire, an oceanographer, an actress, a mother, etc., etc.

You are not a teenager, any more than your mother is a mother or your father is a father. Those are what you do; roles you are expected or choose to play. But when you think that's all you are, that will be all you are! And none of those roles is enough. Otherwise, doctors, housewives, admen, etc.,etc., wouldn't be going to psychiatrists to find their selves.

The advantage of knowing there's something more to you than the roles you play is that it produces *self*-confidence; a very good thing to have. People who lack *self*-confidence are always trying to prove themselves to others. And the ways they try to prove themselves is to get control of others' egos—through wealth, physical or political power, with tears, laughs, etc., etc..

Nothing to prove
The person who knows who he/she is and has come to terms with that reality is not all wrapped up in him/her self; not constantly trying to prove something; not always feeling threatened and poorly treated. They don't have to be concerned with what other people think of them.

It is the rare person who is unconcerned with impressing. Yet you cannot be you while trying to impress somebody else. You can't really hear what somebody else is saying if you're thinking about what they are thinking of you. Even if your method of impressing is being a 'good listener,' it's superficial listening; it's listening with an ulterior motive. When you are confident about your place in the sun —i.e., being 'centered'— rather than dependent on the opinion of others, you can then concentrate on others instead of what will impress them. That is what really impresses other people—being totally interested in them. You can only do that when you aren't concerned about your own status. Most of us spend our lives reacting to others. Until we come to terms with our own self-worth, we're going to have problems relating to others. Face it: belonging to a gang; dressing according to the latest fad; disliking someone because of their color or accent—people like that are seeking the approval of others.

Homo sapiens is a gregarious species; that is, we enjoy social intercourse. So 'belonging' (to a neighborhood, a school, a band, a church, etcetera) is perfectly natural. It becomes unnatural when those little societies feel the need to dominate or 'put down' those who don't belong. An insecure individual is an object of pity. When they form a group—beware.

Fulltime confidence

Being confident of one's ability to be a high-jumper or a lawyer or a cook is fine, but it's a far cry from having *self*-confidence. You're only a cook/lawyer/high-jumper, etc., part-time. That doesn't produce full-time confidence. You've probably heard your mom complain about "having no time to be me." What she's really saying is, "Who am I?" That lack of *self*-identity is what's behind the rush to discover "me" via consciousness-raising movements. (Some people beg the question by losing their *self* in cults.) The truth is, you will feel inadequate, threatened and off-center until you have a focus, an anchor, a *self* to be. Again, there's no *self*-identity to being a mother or a millionaire. Those are just titles; experiences.

Beyond brains and brawn

What you are transcends any time or place, group or title. Essentially, *you are realizations.* To be sure, you also are sensations, emotions, thumbs, nerves, brains and brawn. But those are your media, the equipment your consciousness employs to express itself on the physical plane. Realizations are manifestations of pure super consciousness; that which produce insight, private inner experiences dependent on no outside cause. The essential, inner you can function independent of the outer you; that is, it needs no body to realize itself. If you'd like to experience this state of no-mind without fooling with psychedelics or spending months chanting in a Tibetan monastery—struggle into a wet suit, suspend your self in a tank of body-temp water breathing through a mouthpiece. Cover the eyes so no light can touch them, and the ears so no sound that reach them. When your senses have nothing to sense you experience an incredible ecstasy. Total completeness, total togetherness, total security, total desirelessness. For those moments you are pure consciousness seemingly detached from your mortal coil. The realizations that come to you in this state are not generated by physical stimulus, nor do they start in your brain/intellect. They must pass through that system, your bodyworks, but they don't start there. Returning to the world of weights and measures, sounds, smells, tastes and feels—you will realize how that body of yours only makes things difficult, gross and confusing. But most of all you would realize that the body is baggage (however necessary it is for this trip), that you can and will continue to be you without it. A rather sensational piece of information!

A preacherman no doubt would say 'soul' is the purest essence, but let's not get hung up with words. It's your 'center' place ... it's no place and every place. It's the Big Mystery. But it's no mystery how to use this source of All.

Notes to My Self

Notes to My Self

3

THE
TWO REALITIES
OF LIFE

*"There are more things in heaven
and earth, Horatio,
than are dreamt of in your philosophy."*
— William Shakespeare

F air warning: What follows isn't going to come
easily. But some understanding of the concept
revealed here is basic to the chapters dealing
with nitty-gritty issues like sex, drugs, teenage
blues, career choices and so forth. So fasten your
seat belts ...

You live in two 'worlds,' within two different planes
or realities. (Most people don't know it, but that
doesn't change what-is.) There's the dense world of
material realities. And the space-y world that is difficult (for sense-oriented people —i.e., most of us!) to
witness. Included in this difficult-to-see/touch/hear
world are things like energy waves or vibrations, such
as those that carry light and sound.

The seen and the unseen

Even if you acknowledge the presence of both, it's still tricky to keep these two realities straight. That's because we operate in both worlds simultaneously. Our conscious self is of one; our physical self of the other. For most people, only the seeable, touchable, hearable, tastable, smellable is real. So we are constantly being confused by mysterious, unseen happenings.

It's important to keep the two realities in balance. But not easy. One is always trying to dominate the other. So people tend to be totally devoted to the physical facts of life or completely immersed in the metaphysical. (That's why mystics are usually found far removed from cities, and why they're surrounded by devotees who feed them and shoo away tigers and vipers.)

Making possible what seems impossible

The so-called material world, the one bounded by your five senses—let's call that 'Reality I.' Here's where things are hot and cold, heavy and hurtful, sweet and sour. It's when you tune-out the low frequencies that radiate from material objects and tune-in to high vibrational levels that things get interesting. This is the phenomenal, miraculous world where the seemingly impossible becomes possible. Let's call this 'Reality II' where you get to create your own experiences unbounded by physical limitations.

The higher or super-consciousness can motivate the body to outdo itself, producing exceptional feats or what athletes call 'peak performance.' This level of consciousness can do even more amazing things when it detaches from the body: it can travel in time and space, mentally move or alter objects. Just because the scientific establishment can't reproduce such phenomena in a laboratory doesn't mean it can't happen. It simply means it is presently beyond present-day science. But remember, yesterday's miracles are today's science.

You see, all our reference points are relative to Reality I, the material or physical plane. When we talk about something being impossible (like out-of-body experiences, extra-sensory perception and other psychic phenomena), we're referring to what is observable to our gross sense of sight, touch, smell, etc. Walking through a brick wall is, in fact, impossible relative to our material form. However, our awareness or consciousness can pass through that wall to experience what's on the other side, to communicate with what's there.

The confusion produced by these two realities has produced some legendary misunderstandings. Like the Sermon On The Mount: Jesus was directing that lecture to some pretty enlightened souls, his Disciples. So he was speaking to an elevated consciousness operating on the Reality II level. But when Jesus' advice was carried down the mountainside to the world of

Reality I, its application caused all kinds of mischief. The Hindus have a parable about this sort of thing: *There was once a holy man who came to a village. The villagers warned him that he must not go along a certain path because a venomous snake which had killed many people lay there. "It won't hurt me," said the holy man, and continued in the direction of the snake's abode. Sure enough, the snake approached, reared its head ready to strike, but when it saw the holy man it prostrated humbly at his feet. The sage taught the snake to give up the idea of biting and killing, whereupon it slithered off to its hole to pray and meditate while the holy man proceeded on his way. Knowing that the snake was now harmless, the boys of the village would attack it with sticks and stones whenever it emerged from its hole. After a time the snake grew so weak from its injuries that it could scarcely crawl.*

When next the holy man came to the village, he heard about the snake's condition. Going to its hole, he called it forth. Hearing its teachers voice, the snake came squirming out crippled from the blows it had received and terribly thin because it was not getting enough to eat. The holy man questioned the snake about its condition. "Revered sir," the snake replied, "you asked me not to harm any creature so I have been living on leaves. Perhaps that is why I am so thin." Having developed the virtue of forgiveness, the snake had forgotten the boys who had almost killed it. The sage said, "No, there must be a reason other than want of food that is responsible for your condition. Try to remember." Then the snake replied, "Oh yes, some village boys beat me, but I wouldn't bite them. I just lay silently and suffered their torments." The snake expected to be praised for resisting evil. To its great surprise, however, the holy man became quite cross. "How foolish you are," he cried. "I told you not to bite. Did I tell you not to hiss?"

So when you operate on the material Reality I level, as you are, you must contend with sticks and stones. You've got to know when to 'hiss' and when to turn the other cheek.

Hissing should be the next to last resort, before striking out. If you know when and how to hiss, you may never have to strike! Once violence is resorted to, whether defensive or not, you lose. People who fight have been defeated before the first blow is struck. They have lost their humanity and retreated to their animal past. Hissing is somewhere in-between. It's a way of saying, "Watch it—I'm capable of being a viper; don't mess with me." That's why peace-loving nations arm themselves: to keep the peace.

Play a happy tune and happy dancers will join you
Before hissing, try smiling. A smile can be very disarming. Not a thin, little nervous smile, and certainly not a smartass smirk, but a great big open, confident smile that says "I'm okay, you're okay." It's really hard to be mad at or suspicious of someone who wears a happy, smiling face.

Getting along in this me-against-you Reality I world is real simple if you're a one-dimensional person who sees everything in simple terms of good/bad, win/lose, black/white. This kind of person considers life a great big contest: capitalism versus communism, Christianity versus pagans, North versus South, our school versus your school, American products versus Japanese products, rich versus poor, Us versus Them. Power is the sole concern of this mindset. It's a hangover from our hunter ancestors (when 'kill or be-killed' was the law—jungle version). There's a little Tarzan in all of us. But Tarzan is closer to man's past than our future.

Two ways to go

The two realities do seem to complicate your journey through life. They offer alternative routes. You arrive at the junction when you reach the teens. Both routes are parallel, heading in the same direction (to the 20's, 30's, and beyond). But Reality I might be seen as the lower road, where the body/ego finds its physical needs and pleasures fulfilled: eating, drinking, sex and such. The high-way takes you into the metaphysical realm where you'll find inspirational pleasures such as music, literature, meditation and the like. Teenagers usually follow the physical route, at least to start with. In time you'll learn to travel both roads, switching back and forth. (Some people manage to follow both routes simultaneously!)

Unfortunately, at our present stage of evolution, most humans have only a faint acquaintance with their higher consciousness, so the ego usually dominates and we spend most of our lives acting like Ivan The Terrible. That faint little inner voice peeps through on Sundays and at Christmastime, and when we're alone, especially before falling asleep (if we don't go to bed with the radio dominating our consciousness).

Because what you do is often in conflict with how you feel, you accumulate a lot of guilt. Some of us get rid of it in a confessional manner: private, ritualistic or psychiatric. Others resolve the conflict by shutting off the conscience: they drown that inner voice with a calliope of TV, radio, drugs, booze, sex, violence. What a pity.

Two is better than one

Reality I and II need not conflict. Being a moral, compassionate, tolerant, joyful person doesn't doom you to failure or ridicule. A pretty good definition of a 'together' person is one who keeps both realities working harmoniously. Those are the people who seem to "have everything" going for them: they're good at sports, good fun, good students—everything seems to come their way, everything works for them. It's as if they have an extra power source, two engines instead of one ... which is about right! Reality II can make Reality I better. It isn't just somewhere to hide from the nasty, hard-edged world; it sharpens the tools you dig with, stimulates peak performance. The idea is to apply Reality II *principles* to Reality I *practices*— the same as some Christians apply the Golden Rule ("Do Unto Others ...") in business dealings. It pays. Feels good, too. Also, if you know you're of the Cosmos, it's a lot easier to overcome fears of failure, an unpleasant environment, a lousy school, cruddy clothes, a funny nose.

Still, nobody's perfect at juggling the two Realities; even Jesus had a few bobbles. When that happens, don't quit. Pick-up and start again. Practice makes perfect. That's what you're doing here—practicing.

Notes to My Self

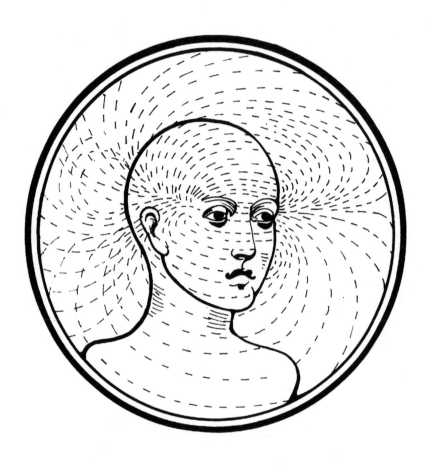

4

HOW DO YOU KNOW YOU KNOW?

*Stop talking, stop thinking and
there is nothing you will not understand*

There's only one way to know something; that's to experience it. Somebody can tell you why it's impossible to walk through a brick wall, and you may accept their reasons without experiencing a flat nose. But when you take somebody's word for anything, you don't *really* know. You are just accepting or agreeing. Obviously, we can't seek first-hand experience about everything. We've got to take somebody's word for a lot of things. If Boeing's chief test pilot says the plane will fly, we are inclined to accept that and buy a ticket.

Knowledge versus wisdom

'Knowing' that comes by means of agreement is what you call 'knowledge.' Knowing that results from personal experience is the basis of wisdom. So a

31

knowledgeable person is not necessarily a wise person.

We get most of our knowledge about ourselves via other people ... from the way they experience us. If the teacher say's you are dumb, you figure you must be because teachers are smart. So you play the dummy role. If you never spend any time experiencing your self, then all you will ever know about your self is what you see mirrored in other people's opinions, desires and fears. You become a reflection of these second-hand perceptions.

Monkey see, monkey do

We've already established that the face you show others has little to do with the feelings that operate behind that face. It's as if you went out dressed in a monkey suit and got your self locked up in a zoo. If all you are is what other people see/experience, then you're stuck with your act. If we shed our monkey suits —or however you dress your ego— we come face to face with what's inside. To do this consciously, without resorting to psychedelic chemicals*

• •

* Psychedelics can be a shortcut to experiencing who or what we are. Nobody who has ever used psychedelics thinks all they are is a physical package. But be warned: To suddenly, without proper preparation, experience your self apart from your fleshy facade can be quite a shock— especially during the teen years which are a kind of shock treatment. That's why psychedelics are nothing to fool with; they can leave you disoriented and unable to regain your psychological balance. There are safer, more righteous ways of experiencing your 'I Am.'

requires some effort—like meditation. You've got to get your body/ego out of the way; the objective being—to stop thinking about you and all the things that affect you; to vacuum the inside of your head *to quiet the mind.*

The Western world resists 'mystical' things like meditation because, according to our values, to stop thinking is to stop functioning... to stop being human! Thinking is our pride and joy (though in fact it too commonly is the source of our miseries). Shutting down the cerebral cortex —the brain's thinking generator— is related to going out of our mind. But that is where you must go to get to higher levels of truth. There are all kinds of techniques for developing this ability—such as bio-feedback and do-it-yourself meditation.

Probably it is asking too much of a teenager to retreat from the physical/thinking world once a day ... to be quiet and still and spend some private moments floating in Reality II. But it is worthwhile to learn how and why it's done, so that in later life you know how to shut out the insanity of the material world and recharge your batteries by plugging into the cosmic power plant.

Meditation, or even daydreaming, is very beneficial, but that doesn't mean you must do it or else. If you aren't curious; if you don't feel any great need or desire to switch off Reality I—forget it. If you don't have the motivation, it will never happen anyway.

And for most people the motivation comes later in life when the head gets cluttered with crap: fears, anxieties, disappointments, regrets and resentments. That's when the need to debug your self becomes a necessity, else the mind becomes so overburdened it may blow a fuse (which is a pretty good definition of a nervous breakdown—Nature's way of making you switch-off Reality I). Anyone who can experience the state of no-thing early in life will never need Nature's shock treatment or the ministrations of cults, gurus or psychiatrists.

Brain, mind, soul, spirit

And in case you've lost track of the connection between meditation and this chapter's title—the link is this: You will never really *know* anything until you know the know-er is not the brain *per se.* And if it isn't the brain —the microprocessor driving your operating system— it must be the so-called consciousness —that which programs your operating software. Just because we can't locate the consciousness with a scalpel doesn't mean it isn't there! A hundred years ago we couldn't locate X-rays, much less radio waves— but they were 'there' nevertheless, waiting to be recognized and utilized. When "mind" is referred to, consider that the interaction of brain and consciousness.

"Soul" and "spirit" are even more difficult to corral with words meaningful to a teenager (with more prag-

34

matic concerns). Any attempt to do so not only would wrinkle your brow while adding nothing to the subject at hand.

No exits

Don't get the idea that just because Reality II is a higher (on the vibrational scale) level of reality, you should excuse your self from Reality I, by whatever means. No, no, no, no, NO! We are not here to deny we are here. So forget about hiding behind a smokescreen of dope and booze, much less acid, or any of the other stuff that changes or distorts the hard realities. People who drop-out aren't getting out. It's no way to escape. It's a deadend—meaning you'll have to return to 'Go' sooner or later.

The only reason you should know about the knower —your higher consciousness— is because it helps you operate in the so-called 'real' world of Reality I. It helps you soar like an eagle over the badlands below. Knowing the knower, that private inner you, is tied to the eternal creator of the cosmos gives you a lift; a big boost that raises you above the ego traps of drugs, violence, wealth, ad nauseam. Knowing is half the battle. Doing something with that knowledge is the other half.

Notes to My Self

Notes to My Self

5

OPPOSITES

Life is a pendulum that swings back and forth

Y ou can't be wealthy unless someone is poor. You can't recognize beauty without seeing ugliness. There is no light without dark, and objects require space to be perceived as solids. Birth is inconceivable without death, as is summer without winter. Good requires evil., and vice versa. Every coin has its reverse side; every 'plus' is offset by a 'minus;' and every action produces a reaction. That's really all there is to the so-called 'facts of life.' All else flows therefrom: masculine/feminine, young/old, meek/ bold, winners/losers. There could be no sadists without masochists. No doves without hawks. No yin without its yang.

A world in which everyone is rich and everyone is beautiful is unimaginable. How would you know who is rich? How would you know there is such a thing as rich? Losers, ugliness, evil all serve to make their opposites possible.

The unexplainable explained

This is not wordplay or a lot of obscure fluff. Opposites or dualities may be a paradox (a good word to look up in your dictionary as you'll wrestling with paradoxes for the rest of your life), but they also explain what otherwise would be inexplicable. It's the philosopher's key; a poetic form of physics. When you come to realize losers fulfill a necessary function (they make winners possible!); that some people are attractive because others are not—then you will never be confused by the presence of 'bad' things in a perfect Universe created by a loving God.*

If nothing was imperfect, there could be no perfection

How could you conceive of God as perfect if He/She/It did not reveal imperfection for purposes of contrast? It makes no difference if you substitute 'Allah' or 'Nature' or a 'Greater Power' for 'God.' Whatever you wish to call the originating, primordial creative force, the source of all energy, 'It' created a perfectly balanced Universe. The balance is a product of equal and opposite extremes. The rhythm of life is

● ●

* "I am Lord not of light alone but of darkness also ... I the Lord destroy with darkness. But with darkness I also create. The wise discern this. Fools deluded by outward appearance create a web of their follies."—Book of Tokens

created by ups and downs, highs and lows. Everyone has both. Everyone *is* both! One leads to or produces the other.

Everything and everyone is a combination of qualities
There is nothing to do with this rhythm except to just realize it. It is what accounts for life's inconsistencies, among other things. Yet despite being surrounded by evidence of this, we still expect people to be consistent and average; to be always good or always bad. We actually become irritated when someone we love to hate does something nice. Either we don't believe it, or we resent it. "How dare you act nice after being hateful so long? What are you trying to do, confuse me just to be mean?"

It is all too possible for a clergyman to mount the pulpit and inspire his flock with great spiritual wisdom on Sunday and come Monday be arrested for lewd conduct unbefitting the Ministry. What's disturbing about that isn't lewdness *per se*, but that it was a Minister being lewd! People can't handle opposites such as 'lewdness' *and* 'minister.' So either we just won't believe he was exposing himself in the park or we reject his ability to preach and become uninspired about his sermon. That's dumb. Why throw the baby out with the wash? Why reject a good side when a bad side shows itself? That's when we should be charitable, balance the good against the bad instead of going to the extremes that happen when you ignore one side and concentrate of the other. We want the pendulum to swing to one side only. Pendulums don't work like that, nor do humans.

Justice requires patience

Life is a constantly unfolding, ongoing process involving the entire (unimaginable) Universe. We only see people and events in the perspective of our tiny tick of time. And so it may appear that crime sometimes pays, that tyrants often triumph and all manner of wrongdoing goes unpunished. That's because we rush to judgement. We expect to see 'right' prevail here and now, while we are watching. This is wandering a bit from the 'rule of opposites,' but as long as we're off-course for the moment, let's continue the detour long enough to note that our system of temporal justice is represented by counter-balanced scales—the purpose of which is equality; equal rights and justice fairly weighed. But that kind of balance is more theoretical than actual; more a goal than a reality. Perfect justice is delivered on the cosmic scale and in the Reality II sphere. In this world of form and function, bodies and intellects are unequal. People really do suffer injustice in Reality I.

What goes around comes around

People of color (brown, yellow, red or black) have it tough in a white-dominated culture.* The scales are always tipped in one direction or the other. Because colored minorities are discriminated against by the white majority, Affirmative Action legislation gives them certain compensating advantages which discriminate against the majority. And around and around we go. Workers are exploited by capitalists which causes them to unionize which drives the capitalists out of business! Too much of one thing produces too much of another thing.

The fact that representative government endeavors to keep things equal and fair by law and moral persuasion is an honorable undertaking but destined to produce unequal results. When one side prevails, the other side seeks undue advantage. Nevertheless, it is a noble effort that distinquishes mankind from other life forms. Plants, beetles and frogs show no concern for their less fortunate brethren. On the other hand, the plant and animal kingdoms are incapable of prejudice and hate. Only man (and perhaps some mammals) demonstrate compassion, the ability to put your self in somebody else's space ... to feel what they feel, as if you were linked (which, of course you are, per Chapter 15).

●●●●●●●●●●●●●●●●●●●●●●●●●●●●●●●●●●●

* What should those who suffer from this (or any other injustice) do about it? On the Reality I level, they should do everything of a positive, constructive nature to change the consciousness of their oppressors—such as voting. On the Reality II level they should endeavor to follow the way of the yoga: " When man is bad, do not hate him. Any thought of hate, even so-called 'righteous hatred' is evil; will raise a wave of hatred and evil in our own minds, increasing our ignorance and restlessness. Sin exists only in man's eyes; (merciful) God does not look to man's sins." Easier done when observing oppression than when suffering from it. But that is the path we must seek.

To have and have not

The rule of opposites also is what causes us to covet the things we don't have. The person who lacks wealth desires money. Career women want families and housewives want independence. The sailor dreams of settling down on a plot of ground while the farmer wants to put the wind to his back. (More about this follows in the chapter entitled, "Problems.") The lesson here is: you can't have and eat that well-known cake. You can't become full without having been empty. You won't feel joy without knowing sadness. There are two sides to everything in the Reality I world.

Good and bad are relative measures

It should also be recognized that Reality I does not hand out an equal number of 'goods' and 'bads.' As mentioned, some people appear to experience more of the bad than the good. An Untouchable in Calcutta knows only hunger, illness, hopelessness. Or so it would seem from our point of view. But the rule of opposites is a relative measure. When you are very low it doesn't take much of a boost to make you feel high. When you are starving, a crust makes a banquet. A child who has never had (nor seen) a toy can be made happy with a stick and a stone. Such examples are not meant to justify a diet of bread crusts. Why that is one man's fate and not another's is a different discussion. The point here is that 'bad' on your scale might be 'good' on somebody else's. Some people experience poorness on an annual income of $100,000, whereas $10,000 is rich to another. Neither person can imagine how the other is possible.

Notes to My Self

5. OPPOSITES

Notes to My Self

6

RESPONSIBIBLITY AND IRRESPONSIBILITY

If you 'get' this chapter you can close the book and go about your business because you will have all you need to make the most of your teen years ... or any years

The person who takes responsibility for his/her own thoughts and deeds is the person who will never suffer resentments *the worst psychological affliction a person can contract.* Resentment is the one ailment from which there is no recovery ... except by taking responsibility.

How to become a victim

Most of the things that happen to us happen as a result of some easily remembered act or attitude. When Jeff, not a particularly dedicated student, signalled a classmate to show him the answers to a multiple-choice test and the classmate wouldn't cooperate, Jeff glowers and mumbles a threat. The teacher hears and accuses Jeff of cheating. He fails the test, earns a blackmark with the teacher and blames the uncooperative classmate for the outcome. ("The little sh-t wouldn't help me.") So Jeff ends up losing twice. One, got a blackmark on his record and two, he's gained a resentment that blossoms into a poisoned relationship with a fellow student that escalates into a shoving match in the hallway a couple of days later for which Jeff is blamed by an observing teacher. Now he's in bigger trouble and, of course, he blames the 'innocent' classmate ... all of which Jeff could have avoided by taking responsibility for trying to crib those answers in the first place. All he has to do is realize who did what. Admit it to himself. That's all it takes. That unravels what has become a complicated problem and Jeff doesn't carry the burden of resentment into all his other affairs. Make no mistake, blaming others —making your self a victim—becomes a habit that will produce cancerous consequences throughout your entire life.

How to make a bad situation worse
Another example: Bridget, 16, goes out on a school night to study at a friend's house down the block. She agrees to be home no later than 10:30. Some boys drop by around 9:30 and they decide to make a Big Mac run. One thing leads to another, it gets to be 10:30, but Bridget doesn't want to be a wet blanket. When they finally pull up in front of her house, it's past 11. Her mom spots the car and the boys, leaps to conclusions and jumps all over Bridget who, of

course, feels she did everything reasonable to get home as promised, and in any event, she was an innocent victim of circumstances beyond her control. So Miss Prissy's reaction is to slam her bedroom door in mother's face—which makes an already angry parent more so. Hearing the commotion, father enters the scene. Through clenched teeth he tells Bridget she's not to step foot out of the house at night for one month. Bridget screams, "I hate you. You're awful," and the next few days are miserable for everybody.

Wouldn't it have been easier for Bridget to allow she was late and regret it? It *was* her responsibility, whatever the unexpected difficulties. And it was her decision to go along to MacDonald's however harmless and reasonable that seemed at the time. Had she reacted to her mom's over-reaction with that opening acknowledgement, her mother would have calmed down, listened to the ensuing story and in the end probably sympathized with Bridget. After a for-the-record, "Don't do it again," her parents would have walked away from the matter and everyone could have gone to bed wearing a smile. No lies, no personal compromises or giving-in, and no on-going resentments.

It works

Taking responsibility for whatever happens to you is right simply because it makes your life work better. True, sometimes it isn't clear where you went 'wrong.' A lot of un-good things happen that don't appear traceable to any doing of yours. Well, too often that's just your ego's defense mechanism working to protect itself. Most times, if you hunt hard enough, you'll discover you created the cause that produced the effect—however delayed it was manifesting itself.

Hindus, among others, perceive tragedy (ill fate that befalls the seemingly innocent) as the harvesting of acts committed in a previous existence: your karma. But most often you don't have to go back that far. Maybe beyond last month. Maybe as far back as your childhood. But somewhere back there is the seed of what is being harvested today.

15-billion years without a hitch.

That's how the Universe works: with perfect consistency. That's the only way it can work. If an effect had no cause, or an action produced no reaction, the whole Universe would go "Tilt" and self-destruct. The fact that it hasn't over the past 15-billion years or so indicates everything is in perfect working order. Maybe you have decided not to like what's happening to your body and ego right now. That's *your* responsibility. But the Universe keeps its equilibrium whether or not it's to *your* liking.

The two parts that make all creation work so perfectly are, as mentioned, cause and effect. You can't have one without the other. Also, as mentioned, effects don't always have identifiable causes. But that

doesn't mean there isn't one. It just means you can't
or won't comprehend it. In that case, accept it. When
something goes amiss in your life, accept at face value
that you are the cause of it. One, it's true. Two, you
escape all those personally disturbing feelings that
come from blaming it on parents, teachers, classmates,
Republicans, immigrants, cops, the Devil, Fate, the
weather, *ad infinitum.*

Poor little me

People who hang onto what they judge to be in-
justices are crippled by them. *"How could they have done
that to me ...'" "What did I ever do to deserve that?" "I was
quietly minding my own business when this big pig of a cop
grabbed me..."* No doubt about it, big cops have been
known to walk up to innocent bystanders at a friendly
neighborhood riot and thump them smartly on the
head. And that bystander would be sympathized with
after his release from the emergency hospital if he
felt he had suffered unjust treatment.

But, again—the Universe doesn't assign "unjust"
or "innocent" labels to people and events. In order to
be knocked on the noggin, you had to be in the vi-
cinity of the noggin-knocking. That was *your* choice.
It was a choice that involved risk (as every choice
does!). Even if you couldn't help but be in the middle
of the fracas, you were in fact there. And there's where
you should leave it. But most of us make matters worse
by shouldering the burden of resentment. The hate

for the club-swinging cop carries over to all cops. One more monkey to carry around on your back for the rest of your life. Who needs it? Just say, "Oops! I was there. Turned out to be the wrong place." Then the worst if over. You've got a sore head. You've been inconvenienced. But you aren't crippled with hate. This is not being a doormat. Nobody's recommending you roll over and play dead.

When Jesus advised, "Turn the other cheek ..." he wasn't being holier-than-thou. He was, as usual, being terribly practical. To "suffer the slings and arrows of outrageous fortune" is ennobling. But to "set up arms against a sea of troubles" will surely cause worse troubles. (Just ask Hamlet.)

Judge not

Human beings cry out for justice, and it is there. The Universe, God—call it what you will—metes out perfect justice. You don't have to play judge. Trust the atom and the galaxies to serve you properly. If you choose to head up river without a paddle, don't accuse the river of making it tough.

Nobody suffers self-pity like teenagers. If it's any consolation, it would appear you are the victim of forces beyond your control. Somebody else does appear to physically run your life. You are burdened with expectations you didn't ask for. But don't get suckered in to feeling sorry for your self. You'll pay a price for blaming anyone but your self.

Blame not

'Blame,' of course, is a value judgement that you'd be better off not to make. When you blame somebody or something, you are in effect saying you are helpless; a victim of circumstances beyond your control, because you cannot control 'them' or 'it.' If you've got a gun maybe you can control somebody's physical movements, but not their spirit—not their thoughts and feelings.

On the other hand, when you take personal responsibility for something you've judged 'bad,' that puts you in the driver's seat, in control. *Only you can do something about you.* That's all you can do. That's all you need do. (If each and every person cleaned up his or her own act, nobody would be messed-up ... it'd be Heaven On Earth.)

So self-pity, resentment, injustice are cop-outs; ways to avoid the responsibility for running your own life. (And if you don't run it, somebody else will!)

The plus side

As usual, it's easier to describe how something works in the negative than to give it a positive spin. But taking responsibility has its plus side—it's not just a way of reconciling or removing problems. Taking responsibility also is taking credit. When something good happens to you, it's no more 'Good Luck' than bad things are 'Bad Luck.' You are the cause of those good things. You deserve whatever good fortune comes your way. Even if you stumbled onto buried treasure while chasing a butterfly. You were there. You made it happen. Enjoy.

Notes to My Self

Notes to My Self

7

HAD ANY
GOOD FANTASIES
LATELY?

"We are such stuff as dreams are made on."
— William Shakespeare

Making believe' is usually connected to daydreaming, and daydreaming is usually linked to time-wasting, the opposite of *doing* or *achieving* something worthwhile. And yet it is the act of making one's self believe anything is possible that makes anything possible.

Dreaming of becoming a millionaire (a commonplace fantasy in today's culture) is a necessary part of wanting to ... which is essential to becoming one. Making believe you are scaling Mt. Everest is a necessary preliminary to *doing it*. It's the first part; what goeswith creating the desire and acquiring the ability. Because you in fact can become a millionaire or a mountain climber; *the difference between wanting and becoming is desire.*

The reason adults dig themselves into ruts is because adults stop 'making believe.' That's because 1) they don't take the time, thinking it a waste of time, and 2) as people get older, their options are reduced; that is, a 40 year-old can't become a millionaire before 30, an Olympic high-jumper, or a fighter pilot. After 40, these 'can nots' become so numerous they tend to obscure the 'can dos.' But the 17-year-old can be most anything he/she wants to be. And making believe is part of making those dreams/desires/wishes come true.

How dreams come true

There's a metaphysical principle at work here, called the Process of Affirmation. But there is no need to formalize a simple procedure. Just let your mind visualize the object of your desire. *Treat it like it has already happened.* If being a singer is your dream, dream of appearing before a sellout concert, or accepting a Grammy, getting a Gold record. See your self in recording sessions, being mobbed by adoring fans. Of course after dreaming must come some effort developing the necessary skills and sharpening your talent. But as mentioned, daydreaming will generate doing-something-about-it. The concept has to precede the reality.

How this principle or process works is really not important. But because our technological society teaches that understanding must precede believing, let's try to describe mind-power in simple terms.

First of all, there is the practical matter of capability and probability. A 7-foot 300-pounder isn't destined to be a jockey. Or the probability of you amassing a larger fortune than Bill Gates before you're 20 is too slim to make it worth dreaming about. But if you possess the potential to actualize your fantasy—dream on. What prevents people from realizing their dreams or potential is appearances. Seeing an accomplished pianist flay the keyboards is apt to cause the would-be piano player to think, "Wow, I could never do that." A kid who dreams of flying a Jumbo jet might think twice after surveying the cockpit of a 747. " Gosh, I could never figure-out all those switches and dials." It's the negative thinking, of course, that does the preventing. Appearances trigger the thinking. Thinking you can't or won't plants a can't/won't chip in your memory bank that your microprocessor is programmed to convert into actions of the negative kind. Over time, negative thoughts produce negative results. Successful thoughts engender successful results. Simple as that. (A guy named Norman Vincent Peale turned this rule into fame and fortune with his classic book, *The Power Of Positive Thinking*, the same stuff that supports the Christian Science belief and 'New Thought' churches like Science Of Mind and Unity.

Programming your body
When it comes to physical prowess—things like skiing or tennis, for example—negative thinking pre-

vents the body from doing what's right (what comes naturally). There are no mysterious forces at work here. Thinking you can't or thinking it's hard literally binds the muscles, screws-up your timing and coordination. You actually can think your self into a bind. But instead of seeing your self being awkward and failing, visualize your self going through the serving or schussing motions—so when the time comes to act out your fantasy, your body will know what to do. It really will! It's been programmed with the right moves. Then it becomes just a matter of letting it happen in practice; of not letting your mind interfere by sending the body failure instructions. You've got to believe you can do it not only beforehand but while you're doing it. That involves picturing the outcome: where you want the ball to go rather than how to get it there. For if you were to break-down a tennis serve into its component parts, you'd become hopelessly tangled in herky-jerky movements. It's enough to know what the proper service motion looks like, so you can see your self looking like that.

Granted, this is an oversimplification. You can't 'think' your self into Wimbleton. Practice makes perfect. But employing this advice will help you reach the point much more quickly where results provide the incentive to practice. Most people don't take-up diving or piano-playing or open-heart surgery because of the agony of becoming. But visualizing the ecstasy of being counters that. Athletes as well as performers actually practice using their 'mind's eye.'

"Act the way you'd like to be
and soon you'll be the way you act"

This Process of Affirmation can help you attain any goal so long as it is specific enough to permit 'seeing' your self doing it or getting it. It can help you win the affection of that certain girl or boy. It can help you get a certain car or house or job. Because if you can imagine it, the reality will follow. You will begin doing the right things, being in the right places, associating with the right people that will lead to the right result. It's a matter of receptivity and self-confidence. Conditioning your mind and body to make the necessary moves. The same way we condition our selves to fear and fail.

Now is the time

It's much easier to do this at 15 than, say, 45, when so-called 'reality' makes daydreaming the last resort of fools. So leave your self some time for this important pastime. Bedrooms and hilltops are great places for daydreaming. And don't hesitate to surround your self with objects connected with your desires, such as posters of Mt. Everest, books about mountain climbing and that sort of thing. It's all about using Reality II to control/affect Reality I.

Notes to My Self

Notes to My Self

8

WHY PARENTS
ACT THAT WAY

*"The reason children and their grandparents get
along so well is that they have a common enemy!"*
— Margaret Mead

Before your parents became parents they didn't act that way. When your father is at work, he doesn't act that way. When your mother is with friends, she doesn't act that way. The only time parents act like parents is when they are with you! Just as the only time you act like a son and daughter is when you are with your parents.

Parents fuss and fume, snoop and spoil, nag, love and toil because that's how they perceive parents are supposed to behave.

Parents are people, and like most people they don't like being resisted. When fathers/mothers complain about their kids' sloppy habits, indifference to study, or the decibels your speakers are putting out—he/she just wants to get said what he/she understands fathers/mothers are supposed to say. He/She doesn't necessarily feel good while doing it, but after it's over with, he/she feels better. And that would be the end of it ... if you would merely accept the fact that he/she is just doing his/her parent bit and say something like, "Yeah, I can understand why you feel like that, Dad/Mom." That way he/she knows you heard. You have acknowledged his/her complaint ... without resistance or compromise.

How wars start

But instead of leaving it at that, teenagers feel a need to defend themselves. Some do it with words, some with mumbles, others with a sour, pained look. Well, dammit, all your parent(s) wanted was to fulfill their parental responsibilities and move on to something pleasant. But part of his/her idea of being a parent is to take no smart-alecking from some know-nothing kid. So he/she comes back at you with angry threats ... and away both of you go, around and around, getting nowhere except further apart.

Parents, at least most parents, don't enjoy hassles, nor do they want to dominate. Being a tyrant is a full-time and exhausting job.

Parents, like kids, would prefer to spend their time enjoying themselves, and enjoying you enjoying your self. Parents start acting tyrannical when you oppose them or resist their best efforts to execute the parental role; that is, telling you the 'right' thing to do.

Because society gives parents that right, you are placed in the position of 'going along' or opposing. Of course you don't see it like that. Because most parental advice is not what you want to hear, you get the idea they are against you, anti-you.

Avoiding unnecessary confrontations
There's an easy way to beg the question; to avoid the tension that results from opposition. It works like this: try placing your two index fingers tip-to-tip opposing each other, so they're pushing against each other. Neither gets anywhere The result is wasted energy and frustration. Or, if one finger is stronger than the other, you have a 'winner' and a 'loser.' Neither result is desirable. But if you raise one finger above the other and push, each goes its own way effortlessly. It works with people as well as with fingers. When you stand aside, you haven't retreated, you haven't been compromised or defeated—you've just avoided an unnecessary, unpleasant and unproductive confrontation. That's the end of it.

The point is, parents are not wrong to do what they do anymore than you can be blamed for acting like a son or daughter. And you are not diminishing your self by avoiding confrontations. You're just being wise—wiser than your parents were when they were in your shoes, most likely.

Been there, done that

A few other points about parents. Mothers and fathers have some not-to-be-denied advantages over sons and daughters. First and foremost, every parent has been a teenager. Whereas few teenagers have been parents. So the old folks can (and do) lay the, "I know, I've been there ..." shtick on you. Parents have not only been where you are, they've been where you are going. So they can (and do) add, "... wait'll you grow up, you'll see ..." This one-upmanship never goes over big with a teenager because there's no way to counter. Which, of course, makes you want to try.

The reason for your contrariness is a misguided effort to establish your identity and self-worth. And no doubt about it—it's difficult to assert your individuality and independence when you are 1) dependent on parents for food, shelter and clothing, and 2) subject to a society that gives you no voice in your own affairs. This stimulates various forms of teenage rebellion. And it's why teenagers only feel at-home with their own kind (someone no more than a year older or younger—a very narrow range of friends), and slavishly follow anyone who sympathizes with their predicament: as Dylan and the Beatles did in the '60s, and _____* et al, do now.

• •

* fill-in the blank with whomever it is that speaks/sings for you today.

70

The puberty problem

There are other influences affecting the relationship between parents and teenagers that you can't do anything about except understand them, and in understanding, to be tolerant (knowing you'll be in the same boat when you get a little further upstream). A schism develops between parents and their offspring after puberty. Whether or not your parents know it, or want to be reminded of it, they frequently have difficulty accepting your new-found sexuality. Dealing with the subject on a purely physical plane, the problem is that your sexual development outstrips your emotional and intellectual development (some more, some less). That's what's so awkward about the teen years; you've got the body of an adult, with the same physical needs and desires, but you lack (to varying degrees) the ability to handle it.

Repressing the irrepressible

Imagine the impact this has on your poor parents. One minute you were a totally dependent, trusting, loving little person—and now, suddenly, you look and in some respects act like them! It's not just a sense of loss the parent experiences—it's confusion. Until just a moment ago you looked like a child, and they looked like adults. Now, all of a sudden (to them at least!) the differences have vanished. It's the natural order of things, of course. But to most parents, it is disquieting. Parents often have a hard time handling this new reality. (They can't or don't remember when they were where you are and the effect this had on their parents!) So their usual response is to repress and deny what Nature has provided. Most teenage maladies flow therefrom: alienation, mistrust, shame, frustration, resentment, stammering, furtiveness, grumbling and mumbling.

That's just the way it is. Everyone goes through it. Most get through it without getting themselves so tied up in knots that it takes the next twenty years or so to straighten themselves out. If it wasn't such a tricky business, there'd be no need for books like this.

A school for parents?

There are few jobs in this world more demanding than parenting. No other work involves so many different skills or such a diverse body of knowledge ... to say nothing of patience, forebearance, money and more money. And talk about a commitment of time: parenting is round-the-clock work, seven days a week for 936 weeks without pay. It's a wonder anyone volunteers for the job. And yet there are something more than a billion parents out there. So there must be some rewards and satisfaction involved. But ask what those might be and anyone actively engaged in parenting is likely to answer with a snort.

The fact is, most men and women get into parenting without knowing what they're in for! There are no pre-parenting schools, although there are all kinds of places that teach you how to avoid becoming one. It's a strange business, all things considered.

Perhaps the reason there are so many parents around is because it's so easy to become one (versus *be* one). The becoming part involves doing what comes naturally. Also, every man and woman on God's green earth has an inalienable right to do it, whatever their age, I.Q., religion, political persuasion, morals or means. Because everybody can do it, most everybody does—qualified or not. Most likely you'll do it sooner or later. (Please try to make it later than sooner.)

Some of the world's most celebrated people appear to be piss-poor parents. Success at other endeavors does not a successful parent make! It might well interfere.

What makes a good parent? There are books and books on the subject, but the essential qualities are unconditional **love**, and taking the time to show it. There's no school that teaches parents how to love. Some people have the capacity, some don't. Those who do always find the time to show it.

It depends on the 'luck of the draw' as to who gets what kind of parents, while parents usually get the kids they deserve! Whether or not you think your parent(s) are good, bad or indifferent at parenting— you can do a lot to make them better at it. (Remember, you'll be the first to benefit.) First of all, love them unconditionally, despite your differences or whatever. Everybody responds to that kind of love. Next, follow the advice on the preceding pages. Finally, vow to remember what is was like to be 5, 10 and 15 when you are a parent.

Notes to My Self

Notes to My Self

9

PROBLEMS

*You've got'em. He's got'em. She's got'em.
They've got'em. Everybody's got'em.
Always have. Always will.*

Life is a problem. Life *is* problems. More properly, life is about handling problems. It's like each of us has a certain capacity for problems. Some have a one-quart capacity. Others have a ten-gallon capacity. Whatever it is, it's always full... of problems. When your problem level is lowered briefly because you got rid of a problem, some other problem rushes in to fill the empty space. So don't go around thinking problems are just for now; that after your teen years are past and 'getting-ahead' problems are over with, it's downhill thereafter. The truth is— you carry a full load all the way through life and in the end, you'll die right in the middle of one problem or another.

Don't cringe

This isn't being cynical or pessimistic. Problems don't mean you can't enjoy life. Problems don't exclude fun, sex, sunshine, dignity, spirituality, fame and fortune. Problems aren't even inherently 'bad.' They are 'bad' only if we handle them badly; allow them to do bad things to us.

So it's kind of dumb to resent or fear problems. It's even dumber to think nobody has problems like *your* problems. Of course, it's only human to want to trade yours for somebody else's. (We always want what isn't!) Poor people would gladly trade the problems of poverty for the problems of wealth. Kids would love to have a grown-up's problems, and vice versa.

There are no small problems

This introduces another rule: a small problem is a big problem when it's the only problem you have. Thus it's possible to feel as strongly about your acne as your dad feels about his bankruptcy. Acne is what's happening to you. Going broke is his concern.

Some students of the human condition feel that problems are always with us because they are necessary for growth. Like lifting weights makes muscles grow; handling problems makes your humanity grow. Of course you can grow better (more able to cope) and you can grow worse (less able). So learning how to handle the problems of living is a rather good thing to know. And we won't hesitate to give you a few pointers.

More rules

Before that, let's acknowledge another point of view about why everyone always has problems: Problems are universal because of the way people play the game of life. The rules of the game state that *what-isn't is more important (or desirable) than what-is.* That's because what we are and what we have seems so little, so limiting—whereas what we are not and have not is limitless; an endless shopping list. Being dissatisfied with what-is and valuing what-isn't has at its root a lack of self-esteem. The psychology being, "If *I* have it, it must not be worth much" or "If *I* can do it, it must not be anything special." It's true that a trapeze artist is not amazed at his/her derring-do, anymore than a surgeon is thunderstruck at what his/her fingers can do. We tend to depreciate or take for-granted what we do or have while being terribly impressed or covetous with our neighbors' abilities and possessions. Familiarity does seem to breed contempt.

Discontent explained

You should also be aware that desiring what-isn't requires a knowledge of what could be. Discontent is caused by an awareness of alternatives. It's when you see displays of other people's wealth that your pov-

erty becomes a 'problem.' Which explains why dis-
satisfaction is so rife in this electronic age: instant
communications, especially television, allows millions
of have-nots to see what the 'haves' have. In 1932, an
Alabama sharecropper had little or no contact with
the world beyond his peanut patch. He didn't know
what he was missing. But now he does. Now his kids
do, too. Now every poor person everywhere has their
face rubbed in their poverty or their oppression or
their lousy weather.

This isn't all bad. Matter of fact, being made aware
of other possibilities makes other possibilities possible; it's the very basis of improving the quality of
one's life. You've got to know you're in jail, that there
is an 'outside' before you can gain your freedom. All
the immigration problems the rich nations are experiencing in recent times are due to this. Because the
poor nations usually are populated with brown, yellow and black people while white people own the
rich places, immigration problems become racial
problems.

Old problems

Down through the ages, each new generation has
been confronted with problems unique to that particular time. Until recent times, most of the problems faced by young people involved staying alive
long enough to become old people. A few hundred
years ago, desease and hunger kept the average

lifespan below 40 years. The olden days not only were nasty, brutish, and short; they were also boring for 99% of the populace. If your father was a herder of sheep—herding sheep was what you did forevermore (unless you were conscripted into some Army and went marching off to be slaughtered). If the father was a tradesman or a craftsman; a beggarman or a thief; any son was destined to be one or the other.* There was no escape. Forget about seeking your fortune; fulfilling your destiny. Birthright determined all. Because nothing else was possible; nothing else was expected. So while a guttersnipe may not have enjoyed life in the gutter; there was no anxiety; no stress and frustration —that's a modern day problem, caused by *freedom* of choice.

New problems

Your generation is confronted with its own set of unique problems (what psychologists prefer to call "challenges"); many of them life and death matters. Life today bears little resemblance to life 500 or 1,000 years ago. But death is death; then and now. Then, as now, death was/is the ultimate problem. Only now, the thing that may kill one, may kill everyone: AIDs, a nuclear holacust or melting polar ice caps. Whereas

• •

* Daughters 99% of the time were saddled with a much worse fate: to be married off at 15 or so to some clod of their parent's choosing. They would likely die in childbirth which must have been a welcome reprieve .

people died one at a time in the olde days; these daze whole cities could die in a flash (and in our arsenals we have a flash capable of wiping out all life on the planet... several times!). While each individual can die only once, who wants to die *en masse*? There would be no one left to morn our passing!

In byegone days, a teenager's problems were the same as an adult's because in those days teenagers were middle-aged: they worked like adults; went to war like adults; married and raised children like adults. So a poll of medieval teenage problems would have listed, "food," "warmth," "shelter," "sickness." To see how that compares to your problems, check out the table below:

TOP TEN TEEN WORRIES

❑ Not doing as well as parents (affording an education, starting a career, buying a house)
❑ AIDS
❑ Pressure to have sex
❑ Money or property stolen
❑ Being attacked or beaten up
❑ Being threatened with a gun or other weapon
❑ Being shot
❑ Drugs (for themselves or family member)
❑ Poverty/becoming homeless (caused by adult losing job; family break-up)
❑ Not being able to afford a doctor

Note: these worries were taken from different polls, hence cannot be listed in order of importance.

Every problem is an individual problem. Even if it's a common problem, like drugs, it doesn't feel common to the sufferer. So let's go beyond creating a shopping list of "common problems" and concentrate on solutions.

Notes to My Self

Notes to My Self

Notes to My Self

10

SOLUTIONS

Rx for whatever's bothering you

The title of this chapter may be a bit misleading. Reading this won't rid your face of blemishes, nor will it improve your grades or make the dope peddlers disappear from your neighborhood. (Each of those problems has a solution, but you won't find it here, else this manual would need a few thousand more pages!) This chapter is about techniques for handling problems, whatever they may be.

Okay, so exactly how do you to remain erect while carrying a heavy problem? Number one, don't expect to unload it because, as the last chapter explained, there will always be others to take its place. The person who thinks tomorrow is going to be problem-free is going to be disappointed. Burdens become unbearable when you expect they will soon be off your back—just like 'waiting' becomes unbearable when you expect the wait will be over every next moment. Once you face the fact you'll always have problems, you have reason to develop a posture that will help you bear them effortlessly. When you think you'll be unburdened tomorrow, there's no incentive for learning how to carry a full load through life without becoming distorted and exhausted.

Keep your distance

People who are able to smile in the face of adversity know something. What they know, consciously or intuitively, is that they are above their problems. They don't deny their problems or pretend they aren't serious. A person can be serene even when suffering great pain or facing certain death. People like that have learned to detach their self from their problem(s). Their conscious self seeks refuge in Reality II while their ego self battles cancer or creditors in Reality I.

This has nothing to do with trances or other mumbo-jumbo. It has to do with altering or raising your consciousness by realizing the essential you is separate from the ego you. That kind of detachment allows your consciousness to observe or witness what is happening to the physical you. And as long as you are observing, you're not totally immersed in the problem. Again, this doesn't mean you don't face what is happening, or take the problem seriously. Lots of happenings are mighty serious and awfully painful.

But when you know it's possible to lose a leg without losing any part of the essential, conscious you, then you're no longer attached to the problem; no longer entangled in its web.

Too close for comfort

When you're totally caught up in a problem, so it's all you can think about, you have lost control of the situation. That's what anger does: it makes you lose control of you. You become a leaf in a windstorm.

To witness your self wrestling with a problem (in order to become detached from it) is as simple as discussing it with your self or God—it amounts to the same thing. Do not discuss it emotionally as you would if telling some friend about it. Discuss it like you were not a party to it —i.e., like a third party. That's really all 'witnessing' is. Again, it will not make your problem disappear, but it makes it lighter and bearable; not because of what you said to your self in that discussion, but because you talked it over with your self. That demonstrates there's a part of you that remains apart from the action. Realizing that is all you need 'do.'

Putting theory into practice

All the above comes under the heading of theory. Putting it into practice is what counts. To that end, let's get down to cases and imagine you've been selected to address your school's student body. You agreed to do it several weeks ago when it didn't seem like a big deal. But now, there you are listening to the Principal introduce you to all those kids who've come just to watch you suffer. You start to panic ... your mind races ahead picturing all the ways you're going to embarrass your self. You're convinced your legs won't support you. Your stomach feels like it's going to lose its lunch. Now you're nervous about being nervous! That's called 'losing control,' letting your fears take over. At this point it does no good to know that your ego-self is running the show; that you're afraid of not being admired. You've got only about two minutes to get your self under control. To do that you've got to stop your mind from picturing all the bad things that could happen. You do that simply by experiencing the fact that you're being fearful. You say to your self, "Wow, I'm being afraid. Look at my palms sweat; feel my lips twitching." You notice how your stomach feels. As you experience/witness what's happening to you, it will stop happening in the process. That's because when you are observing your body reacting, you have detached your conscious self from your physical self. Your mind is full of noticing how fear is affecting you, which leaves no room for being fearful! In the middle of noticing or experiencing what's happening, you'll find your self on your feet talking, and the rest will take care of itself. It really works—just that easily.

You can experience away anything that's bothering you. Here's another example. Let's say you're late for an important date. You're on a two-lane country road stuck behind a farmer with a truck load of chickens going 20 miles an hour. There's no place to pass. Your stomach churns. Your head starts to throb. You hate that guy in his rattletrap pickup. You have three choices. Try to pass and maybe kill your self and/or others. Stay in line and get madder as you get later. Or you can decide to experience what is happening to you; witness your self getting mad.. Describe to your self how it's affecting your stomach; how it's making your pits sweat. Inspect your headache: is it a pointed, sharp pain or is it a dull, blunt pain? Is it purple or flaming red? You can't be angry and do something stupid while experiencing your anger. And when you concentrate on what's happening to you (madness), you can't focus on what's going to happen a few minutes from now (late-ness). You've effectively detached your self from the problem.

When you decide to be conscious of your fears, anger and pain, you've got them licked. Mind over matter. Just tell your self what's happening to your self and in the process that happening will either go away or fail to upset you.

Right NOW is always all right
Another cool way to handle the problems of living has more to do with an attitude than a technique.

If you'll stop and think—there are darn few moments when NOW isn't okay. You can be in the middle of a huge problem, like you've just been thrown out of school or you're awaiting trial for shoplifting or your dad's on the way home and when he sees what you did to his car you're going to be grounded for ... ever. But the fact remains, right NOW is okay. NOW is almost always okay. Like right NOW as you read this page. Isn't it okay right NOW? You aren't in pain right NOW, are you? You aren't starving to death right NOW. You aren't being insulted or made fun of right NOW. Maybe it wasn't okay yesterday, and maybe it won't be okay an hour from NOW. But right NOW, there's nothing wrong, right?

You could be flat broke with a heavy date coming up in six hours. If that makes you feel non-okay, it's because you are anticipating a future moment when you won't be feeling okay. But that's not NOW. That will be when you are standing in front of some cash register with empty pockets. And even when that horrible moment arrives and turns out to be exactly the way you feared—that NOW will be filled with activity, you won't be asking your self if it's good or bad. You'll be busy handling the situation. So why let a future NOW spoil a perfectly good present NOW?

We only fear the future

People don't stop in the middle of a gun battle after receiving a bullet in the shoulder and say, "Hey, this NOW sucks." Those few NOWs that are non-okay take care of themselves—they are action NOWs. The NOWs that are noticeable (and ruinable) are the private, passive, contemplative NOWs. And yet those are the moments people use to make themselves miserable by *fearing some future event.* The controllable NOWs are the ones we allow to get out of control. The reason we turn these perfectly good NOWs into miserable NOWs is that we peer ahead, anticipating an expected unpleasantness. We only fear what isn't yet. Like you fear there's a burglar downstairs. If and when you come face to face with the burglar, you'll be too busy reacting to have time for fear. Fear arrives before and fright after the encounter. So *if you don't use your okay NOWs to fear future NOWs, all your NOWs will be okay.* Okay?

Listen up

All this is really very important—well worth serious consideration because teenagers take their problems too much to heart. That's because you haven't had much experience wrestling with unpleasentness. Ten and twenty years down the road you'll have the perspective to realize your current problems aren't the be-all and end-all. But at this point of your life a problem can throw you into a tailspin. That's why so many teenagers are inclined go off the deepend: run away or something worse. So, please—don't treat this chapter like a bunch of hocus-pocus. It's important stuff. It is hoped the methods discussed here have provided a handle you can hang onto in your time of need.

Notes to My Self

Notes to My Self

11

S-E-X

Sex is like Chinese food

Sex, at its most basic/biological level, is devoid of love; an involuntary/instinctive urge producing results no different from those observed in any barnyard. This urge to merge assures the continuation of our species, simple as that.

Wink-wink, nudge-nudge
But S-E-X, as practiced in this day and age, is not as simple as that. In case you haven't noticed, S-E-X is an emotionally-charged subject. Else it wouldn't deserve big capital letters which are the typographic equivalent of "wink-wink, nudge-nudge."

Complicating the uncomplicated
You may well wonder how come something so basic and natural has become so entangled in con-

vention, morals, religion, politics, custom, laws and prejudice ... how come wars are fought because of it, kingdoms have been lost over it, marriages break up on account of it, kids run-away from home and people are put in prison due to it. How could something this spontaneous and necessary become so all-fired complicated? Good question.

The answer involves the sexual process. Early religious leaders were jealous of the ecstasy of sex. They wanted man and woman to procreate but they forbade them to enjoy it. Because people couldn't help but enjoy it, they were made to feel guilty, and turn to the church (with offerings in hand) for forgiveness. Perhaps these early religious leaders weren't total killjoys. Sex and spirituality were/are incompatible (here in the Western world at least). It's the similarities between man and lower animals that's the bother. People don't act human, in the civilized sense of the word, whilst having sex. They act, well—like animals! devoid of all the social graces and proprieties. We do things in the heat of passion we wouldn't dream of doing in any other mode.

One foot in the barnyard, the other in Heaven
It may strike you as inappropriate to discuss sex in context with spirituality because the two don't mix. But that is one reason sex has become such a convoluted, complex, complicated conundrum. Humankind seems to be the only species that strives to

control its animal urges; to transcend the physical realm.

We appear to be in a great tug-of-war with biological or physical needs pulling us in one direction, and metaphysical forces pulling us in the opposite direction. Lower animal forms have no such problem: with them it's all eat, drink, fight, sniff and mate. So far in man's evolution, the physical forces have won most of the tugging contests. This is understandable. Consider that until just fifty to one-hundred years ago, life was a purely physical battle for the great mass of people. Getting enough to eat and drink was the only concern. As more of us move beyond this survival mode, we become 'higher' minded; feel the need to develop our non-physical nature.

It seems to be our destiny to rise above our animal nature, to jettison the weights that keep us earthbound; tied down to the physical plane, a reality humans share with dogs.

Lust and love

Do not get the idea sex is wrong or bad; something to be denied. However, sex that treats the other person like a tree trunk is purely selfish. The funny thing about self-gratification—it never gratifies. Like a Chinese dinner, you keep wondering if you've missed the main course; as soon as you're finished, you're hungry again. When we seek to gratify our physical urges using another person—that is 'lust.' The reason lust is considered unworthy is because it is selfishly motivated.

When lust drives us, we are least discriminating, least compassionate, least patient, least gentle, least human, and ... least satisfied. Men (women, too) lie, cheat, grovel, clown and otherwise reduce themselves to subhuman status to gratify that physical hankering. And yet when it's all over, we feel somehow 'wrong' about it: embarrassed, distressed and compromised. We feel this way not just because society says its bad or any of that. There's no such thing as a bad orgasm, physically speaking. What's wrong about a selfish orgasm is, it's incomplete; it satisfies only our physical half. Our conscious side wasn't invited to the table. It's still hungry for something more.

The best of both

The kind of sex that satisfies both sides of our nature is more properly termed 'making love.' You 'make love' with someone you care about (before and after); someone you can relate to. When the parties feel an on-going affection for each other, the sexual encounter is enhanced by the knowledge that one's partner not only enjoys your body but your 'you.' That's what's behind the female's oft-spoken complaint that " ... men are only interested in my body." What she's trying to tell you, fellahs, is that there is more to her than legs, lips, breasts and butt. When that's all a guy is after—an orgasm ends the relationship. One moment he's acting like a bull; the next he's slinking away like a whipped dog. If the only thing he and his partner had in common was a sexual union—what's there to say or do afterwards? To avoid that awkwardness boys usually find some excuse to get away, which is why some men find it convenient to pay for sex. The person who pays isn't expected to hang around and pretend to care for what's inside the body next to him. It's just 'wham-bam, thank-you, Ma'am."

Coo-ing vs. crowing

What this all adds up to is, 'making love' is better than 'having sex.' Because when there is an on-going affection between the participants —an affection for the way the other person acts, thinks and feels, as well as looks— the physicalness is more intense and the aftermath is beautiful. Our barnyard friends aren't capable of loving—as witness the fact that there is no aftermath when they mate. No snuggling and cooing. The rooster struts away, selfishly crowing about his conquest.

If you have had any sexual encounters (and all the surveys say you probably have), more than likely you've only experienced 'selfish' sex.* So you don't know what 'it' feels like when there's a deep-seated affection twixt you and your partner. The reason you

• •

* You or your partner may proclaim unselfish affection in order to pursue selfish intentions, or simply because it's the cool thing to say/do.

haven't experienced this side of sex is because that kind of affection usually hasn't developed between teenagers. You're too new at having grown-up bodies. You're too full of discovering your own new fully-developed form (and those of your friends). To be blunt about it, you haven't had enough time in the world of grown-up bodies Your consciousness has some catching up to do. This is really what's behind the age-old prohibition against young people 'doing it.' Of course this is an issue that is unreconcilable.

How old is old enough?

Everyone who was ever 16 thought themselves to be 'old enough.' And it's true, that back in the days of Romeo and Juliet, 16 was 'old enough' because people usually didn't live much beyond forty! But now that the actuarial tables predict you'll be around past 80, you have a lot more time to express yourself sexually ... and adults have a lot more reason to advise you to go slow.

Most adults who concern themselves with pro-scribing and enforcing under-age sexual prohibitions may not be consciously motivated by the concerns discussed above. There is, nevertheless, an uncon-scious wisdom at work that leads adults to advise against or disapprove of adolescent sex knowing that it only idealizes the physical experience while ignor-ing the more meaningful/satisfying side. But there's a more critical, impossible to ignore reason everyone

past 21 worries about everyone under 18 acting like
a mink:

Pregnancy
Teenage pregnancy is out of control. We won't
quote a lot of statistics because they'll be out of date
whenever you read this (anyway, you hear them all
the time in sex education and they have absolutely
no effect).

It's really hard to take seriously teenagers' pleas to
be treated like adults, to trust you to do the right thing,
when four out of every ten teenage girls gets impreg-
nated before 18.* 15 and 16 is the most 'popular' age
for pregnant teens. Every one of you knows how to
avoid pregnancy but that doesn't seem to loom large
at the critical moment. When a pregnancy results in
abortion, that's no easy way out. That's physically and
mentally traumatizing. And, depending on your family's
feeling vis-à-vis abortion, it may cause a falling-out that
isn't quickly mended, if ever. If pregnancy results in a
hurry-up marriage—good luck. Some work out, but to
be realistic, you'll be divorced or separated and a single
mother —probably on welfare— for a long time thereafter. If there's no abortion and no marriage, you'll need
more than good luck. Anyway you look at it, your life
will never be the same. That cheap thrill you suc-

• •

* This U.S. statistic is more than twice as high as in industrialized nations
with comporable rates of teen sexual activity.

cumbed to will cost you dearly... you, the child (if there is one), your husband (if there is one) and your future (if there is one) will never be the same. This doesn't mean you can't rise above this trauma and still make the most of your life. But the odds are stacked against you. And not just incidentally, society will pay the bills. All because you couldn't say "No" or take simple precautions. The pill or condoms. Both are best.

Boys will be boys!

What about the guy's responsibilities? What guy is responsible when the fire is burning? Don't depend on it. He'll sweet-talk you, do or say anything to get his way. A stiff p—k has no conscience! Those are just the facts of life. Not pretty or particularly inspiring, but that's how it almost always is. Remember, ladies, *you're the one who is left to bear the burden.* Be selfish. Think of what you have to lose. There is an excellent, straight-talking book on this subject (as well as a related subject: sexually transmitting diseases) available via the order form at the rear. Read and reap.

Sexual preference

Also to be acknowledged in any discussion about sex is the matter of same-sex partners. Talk about an emotionally-charged subject; there are few issues on the social scene that induce more emotion than this one.

It's unclear how many gay people became aware of their gayness while teenagers. By all indications, gayness is a genetic matter* unrelated to upbringing or environment. So if you have homosexual or lesbian proclivities at 25, you were no different at 15. But, because of peer-pressure and society's sanctions vis-à-vis homosexual or lesbian love, most would-be gay men and women don't recognize or won't acknowledge their gayness during adolescence. Some do, but most don't. Those who do usually have a tough row to hoe as teenagers. Those who don't, face a confusing adolescence and a difficult 'coming out' later in life. All of which is a great pity; a real tragedy. There is no fault involved. No decision making. Yet the straight world still operates from the assumption that sexual preference is a matter of choice, or at least can be resisted or changed. That's scientific/biologic claptrap, of course, but that still dominant view causes gay people no end of trouble: it threatens their standing in the community; affects their careers; everything.

This is no place to get into a long discussion about gay life. If you think maybe you are attracted to the same sex and want to know what to do about it— there are all kinds of places you can go for sympathetic counseling/advice/support. Of course there are more of these resources to be found in big cities than small towns; more on either coast than in heartland America. But seek and ye shall find ...

• •

* Parents who are inclined to condem a son or daughter's sexual orientation should remember from whence it came!

Immune Deficiency Syndrome

Today's sexual agenda also must address the AIDS problem. *Problem?* It's a full-fledged disaster! A global catastrophe... the Black Plague of our times.

Christianity's punitive wing calls it, "The Wages of Sin," "Devine Retribution." How mean. How unchristian. Maybe they'll be less judgmental since the disease has crossed the tracks from the gay side of town and now infects the straight community. Until some scientific Lone Ranger rides to our rescue and kills the culprit with a silver bullet—it's going to kill lots and lots of innocent people(along with those who knowingly engaged in so-called "unsafe sex.") And its social side effects—causing young people to withdraw from one another; to become more distrustful, defensive, suspicious, self-pleasing—may leave an even worse footprint on the human psyche. One thing's for sure: AID's looming shadow places a premium on fidelity; self-control; the precaution of protection... and knowing thy partner.

Notes to My Self

Notes to My Self

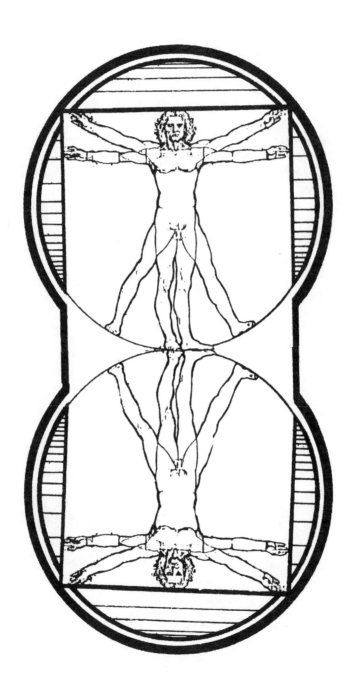

12

HIGHS
AND
LOWS

What are you, a yo-yo?

By all odds you have sixty to seventy more years to live with that body of yours. So any habits you pick-up during your teens are going to hang around for a long, long time. That's one reason it's sad to see teenagers take up smoking, drinking and all the rest.

Right now you are in a discovery period... a time of life when you are emerging from the cocoon of childhood into an adult form. It's a shame to have you take off on your maiden flight with a broken wing. At this moment all your systems are finely tuned: your sense of smell, sight, hearing, your ability to run, jump and be joyful will never again be what they are now. Your present physical high is heightened by a natural psychic receptiveness that makes the teenage years something to celebrate ... and protect.

Everything to lose, nothing to gain

Perhaps it is this unbounded exuberance, this innocent enthusiasm, this eagerness to sample and experiment that leads so many young people to assume they can handle anything. Whatever the reason, the fact is *there is never a time when you have so much to lose and so little to gain by playing around with substances that only bring you down from where you are now.*

Sure, you've got all these frustrations, complaints, problems. If you've been reading along, you know you're no different in that regard. The only thing that's different about teenage problems is that you're better equipped to handle them—you've got the physical stamina, the optimism and the confidence of youth going for you. All the more reason not to introduce unnecessary outside elements into the mix.

That's what inspires this manual: the hope that it might say something that will steer you away from the pitfalls adults have placed in your path. Kids didn't invent booze, cigarettes, cocaine, LSD and the like. Teenagers turn to that stuff with the misguided belief it will either help overcome what's bugging you or make what's good even better.

Save some 'firsts' for later

You can always take up smoking, drinking and drugging any time. You can start next year or in five or thirty years from now. It's always your choice. Try holding out for awhile. Even if you think you're missing something good. If it's good now, it'll be good later. Once you do anything for the first time, it will never be new again. As life moves on, you will be hard-pressed for new experiences. So save a few for later. (You may discover they aren't needed.) Okay, time to lay a few bummers on you. As a convenience to the writer, you'll find pills lumped with pot, booze with tobacco, and horse with coke, although each are separate cases involving different risks and legal sanctions. Anyway, we're not here to discuss the chemistry of THC or the sanity of laws governing its use. One chapter is hardly equal to that. So if you'll forgive an occasional injustice to one or another substance, let's proceed—first from the legal angle.

It is lamentable society has decided to deal with drug abuse as a criminal matter rather than a psychological or medical problem. Actually, that's why drunkenness, dope addiction, lewd conduct and other so-called 'victimless crimes' are crimes. Society finds it much more convenient and comfortable dealing with criminals than it does handling alcoholics, drug users and flashers. But whether the statutes governing the uses of 'harmful' substances are enlightened or not, the penalties are real. And one penalty is unavoidable: The law has caused the marketing of these substances to go underground. And there you are obliged to deal with some pretty unnice characters whose only interest is their own pocketbooks (which they defend at any cost, including your life!)

One of the un-nice services performed by dealers is to turn you on to speed or some new chemical concoction when they are out of grass, or when some big bust drives the price beyond your means. There's no independent marijuana market—it's one big supermarket. You know about supermarkets—that's where people buy on impulse. The only connection between grass and LSD, speed and crack is the marketing connection. Buyers beware.

Double whammy

Addiction is another reality. Addiction is hellish. You have heard all the horror stories, so we'll save you from more of that. All we want to say about addiction is, *"Who needs it?"* There's nothing more precious than 1) freedom: being unattached, free from strings, and 2) good health. When you become attached to anything —drugs, tobacco, alcohol (as well as money, sex, self-pity, etc., etc.)— you have limited your independence, your freedom of choice. Teenagers are always complaining about a lack of independence then turn around and voluntarily stick their head into some drug dealer's noose!

You are no exception

When it comes to addiction, everyone says, "Not *me*," just like every U.S. Marine who stormed the beaches of Iwo Jima in World War II said, "They won't kill *me* ... Tom, Dick or Harry, maybe, but not *me.*" That's the only way the generals could persuade anyone to leave their landing craft — the same way it's the only way you could be sold on amphetamines or heroin. All those dead and dying bodies prove the odds are stacked against you.

Curiosity kills more than cats
The fact is, once you start you've got an excellent chance of becoming someone's yo-yo. As we said early-on, what's sad is you really *don't need* it. You aren't dying for that first drink, or hungering for the first cigarette, or desperate for the first pep pill. You never need the first one! Why go to all that trouble, expense and worry to learn how to need something you don't need? Especially when *the less you need, the freer you are.* As Bob Dylan said a long time ago, "the less you got, the less you got to lose."

Then there is the matter of your physical wellbeing, your health.

Nothing's good without good health
Good health is taken for grant by teenagers who think that's all there is, and it's forever. Maybe you don't know what bad health is like. Sooner or later you will, but make it later if you can because nothing is good when you feel bad. When your body is screaming you don't hear birds singing. Money, sex,

food ... all bodily pleasures turn sour. And it's all the more difficult to handle life's problems when you're feeling crappy.

There's another sort of addiction besides the physical kind. Grass is a good example of this more subtle type of dependence. Marijuana doesn't seem to hook you physically, that is—your body doesn't learn to crave it. It's your mind that wants it. When you become psychologically dependent on anything outside your self to make you (seem to) feel better or more capable, in effect you have given up a degree of *self*-control. Every joint you light is an admission (that registers in your psyche, admitted or not) that your 'you' is inadequate; not good enough. Each and every toke registers as a personal defeat. Just a tiny little chip in your self-confidence, perhaps, but considering the number of years you've got ahead of you— don't be too casual. That's how they cut down giant redwoods, one chip at a time.

Self-confidence is the basic ingredient of self-esteem. When you lack that, you're asking for trouble. (People who have no self-esteem cause most of the trouble; for themselves and others.) And it's pretty hard to get your self out of trouble when you lack confidence and don't like or respect your self. A double whammy.

Crutches don't help, they hinder

The guy who gets drunk to get enough confidence to 'make-out' has just tied drink to sex. It quickly grows into a *goeswith* situation. But the man who says, "It's going to be me who does it, not the booze" is going to increase his *self-* confidence. Even if he's unsuccessful, he doesn't lose what we would have had he 'made it' because of booze. The price you will pay in later life for using alcohol and/or drugs to advance your sex life and general confidence will be an inability to function without them. You will begin using more and more of these 'aids' more and more often until everything you value begins to fall apart. So be awfully wary of using either as a shortcut, or to bypass your emotions, or to heighten pleasure or dull pain.

And what makes you think sights, sounds and feelings are made better/sharper by drugs, much less liquor? What you see, hear and feel *you* see, hear, feel. If a drug can sharpen your senses, you can do the same thing naturally, by conscious effort. All hallucinogenics do is direct or focus your attention. There's nothing they do that you can't do on your own—it's just a matter of deciding to be more conscious of the music; to focus on its colorations and nuances. Drugs just make you more conscious *unconsciously.* Not much self-satisfaction in that. You didn't do it. The drug did. Your 'you' is diminished accordingly.

Because these 'lectures' always come from adults, and because adults are well-known killjoys—teenagers get the feeling that the adult world is anti everything that feels good; that anything good has gotta be bad. Unfortunately, too many grown-ups resent the goodtime orientation of youth. It's a kind of sour grapes attitude ("How dare kids have a good time while I slave away ....") But don't write-off *all* advice that comes from the other side of 30. Jumping off a cliff and soaring like a bird might appear to be a desirable experience to someone who doesn't know about wings and gravity. People who have been around longer than you have learned about falling; so when they see someone heading for a fall, it's difficult not to issue a warning.

Notes to My Self

Notes to My Self

13

KAMIKAZE
KIDS

Teenagers are becoming an endangered species

The teens are a high-risk age: always have been, always will be. But in recent years the risks are getting out of control. In just the past decade, the per capita death rate, accidental or otherwise, among U.S. teenagers has increased by more than 500%.

Learning to fly involves crash landings, true. But your generation of high-flyers are crashing with such regularity that the cause must be something more than bad luck, poor training or faulty equipment. Many crack-ups seem on purpose.

Edgework
Why this flirtation with death? Why are so many teenagers acting like there's no tomorrow—drinking, driving, drugging yourselves into oblivion? And why

now? When life was a lot harder than it is today, teenagers didn't throw in the towel.

Teenage suicide is up 300% in just the last five years. And that doesn't include the kids who've used an automobile, drugs, etc., to kill themselves.

Violence accounts for more than 75% of all adolescent deaths in the U.S. All the statistics show that the United States is one of the most dangerous places in the world for young people. Nine out of every ten young people murdered in the industrialized countries are slain in the U.S. where the homicide rate for ages 15 to 24 is five times that of its nearest competitor, Canada. The number of teenagers arrested for murder in the U.S. has increased 85% over the last three-year period for which statistics were available. Each year nearly a million young people between 12 and 19 are raped, robbed or assaulted. Most of that violence is related to drinking and the drug culture which has been the breeding ground of gangs, those small armies of viscous, alienated, out-of-control kids whose targets almost always are other kids.

Death is permanent

Homicides, whether targeted or aimless, is one problem (with no quick fixes). Even more shocking, depressing and confusing (at least to the adult world) is self-inflicted violence: vehicle accidents, over-dosing, suicides. By definition those deaths were avoidable. If former friends of yours contributed to these statistics—that only makes the loss more tragic. They weren't the victims of some unavoidable virus, a battlefield casualty or stuck down by a bolt of lightning. They didn't have to die. They invited what happened. Driving like a madman tanked up on beer or whatever, scoring drugs in a dark alley—these go beyond risky. It's akin to suicide; slower than a bullet but it hurts more. Of course you know that. But did they? Probably did. There isn't anyone who buys or sell dope who doesn't know they're doing something bad/wrong (which goes to make it good/right in some people's minds). Have you ever met a drunk driver who, when sober, recommended driving drunk? No, most victims knew better. But that didn't stop them.

Is there something somebody could have done that might have prevented all this violence; the self-inflicted kind included? Most of the putative 'cures' fail because they are a quick-fix, dealing with symptoms rather than causes. "Just say no" may make a good slogan, but it doesn't address the reasons teenagers say "yes."*

• •

* Wouldn't you agree that most teenagers say "Yes" to fit-in; to avoid being left out? But in truth, "Yes" is a sign of weakness, an admission you lack the guts and self-confidence to be independent, your own boss and do what you want to do rather than what others want you to do. Teenagers are always moaning about having their lives run by adults, yet when decisions are left to you, you let the crowd decide. Teenagers haven't had much practice saying "No." So before you find your self in a "Yes" or "No" situation—practice saying "No" gracefully, without making a big deal of it. It doesn't have to be a

continued on next page...

Some answers

Ministers, legislators, teachers, various teenage advocates as well as parents keep asking *why, why, WHY* the violent behavior; why the make-my-day ethic that rules the streets and school corridors? The reasons won't much help you to avoid the consequences today and tomorrow. But for the record, they go deep into today's culture: the demolition derbies; films full of blazing guns, exploding cars and heads, bone-crunching, bloodletting sports ... the culture of aggression shows up in our speech, our play and our entertainment; it's cool, it's commercial and it's sickening. It's probably fair to say the root cause begins at home, or the lack of one. The number of single-parent households has skyrocketed: In 1974, for the first time, 50 percent of American children had nobody at home when school let out. Now it's close to 80 percent! Why parents don't stay together, or why both parents have jobs is a whole other discussion. But until these conditions change, or until society finds effective substitutes its going to effect the quality of your life ... and all those who become teenagers after you have made in through the gauntlet.

• •

loud "No" that will cause all the "Yes" people to come down on you. At a time like that, you aren't trying to make them wrong. You're just speaking for your self. If a simple "No" seems too short, try "No thanks, I don't drink." Or if that sounds too negative, try, "I'll pass." Or just say you're having a good time already. (No one can get mad at that!) The point is, have a "No" answer ready. Because people often say "Yes" because they didn't know how to say "No."

Another answer to all the *whys* may be this: More teenagers are being 'burned' (compared to past generations) because today's teens have more matches to play with; all different kinds that burn faster, hotter, longer—all designed by your elders. Twenty-five years ago guns weren't a dime-a-dozen; as common as candy bars. A couple of generations ago dope wasn't so accessible and acceptable ... or as powerful. Fifty years ago automobiles weren't teenage playthings. A hundred years ago this was an agrarian society, while the problems discussed here are most rampant in to an urban-suburban setting.

So don't get the feeling that yours is a failed generation. (If anyone's a failure, it's the generations in front of you.) You and your friends didn't create the conditions that cause more than half of all married couples to divorce. You didn't create the economic conditions that leave the house empty from morning to night and put you in a daycare center during your formative years. You didn't produce the movies, TV and videos that place sexual objects on a pedestal and celebrate wanton violence You didn't invent booze, crack, grass, tobacco, the internal combustion engine, aerosol sprays. And you sure didn't start sex. You just discovered all this.

Every generation has its own set of worries. But unlike generations past, the problems you face are capable of wiping out the future. Nuclear fission remains a threat, whether in the hands of fanatics or stock-piled in underground silos. Biological and chemical weapons are an even worse threat, being easy to manufacture, transport and deploy. Land mines by the millions can turn a pleasant stroll into a ruined life. AIDS lurks under your beds, and melting ice caps threaten to turn your hometown into Waterworld.

These are monumental problems, no doubt about that. But being manmade, they can be solved by man. You aren't going to solve them at sweet 16. Right now all you need do is stay healthy, physically and mentally. The reason you should do that is because *there will be a tomorrow*. No matter how painful the present, you have a lot to live for ... more than you can possibly imagine. And that goes for kids who have it a lot worse than you: teenagers forced to live like animals in an urban jungle, to say nothing of teenagers trapped in African, Middle Eastern and Balkan hellholes. Many of them won't be around when tomorrow comes. At least you have a choice.

What's your choice?

You may choose to stumble through your teen years stoned, like a zombie. You can choose to whine and complain about the mess adults have left for you to clean up. You can lay down and wallow in it, or roll up your sleeves and start improving things. It's your choice: to be part of the problem ... or the solution.

One thing's for sure: Tomorrow will not resemble today. It will not include today's problems. So grit your teeth and hang on for dear life. Soon you'll find your self someplace totally new, with new friends, new everything. Come 21 it's a new ballgame, a fresh start, a whole new race. Those who win will be those who enjoy running. Those who use all their energy complaining usually fall by the wayside, too exhausted to keep up.

Notes to My Self

Notes to My Self

Notes to My Self

.

14

RX FOR THOSE "NOTHING-TO-LIVE-FOR TEENAGE BLUES"

Hope for the hopeless; help for the helpless

He was 16, good lookin,' bright and well-liked. Jason lived in a big house in a small town full of sunshine and affluence. His dad was a honcho, his mom a talented, loving lady. Jason's older brother and sister each had a wall full of athletic and scholarship honors—everything they touched turned to success. Just as much was expected of Jason, maybe more. Oh, his parents didn't push it, *require* it. It was just—well, assumed. The natural order of things. Much of the pressure was his own making. Jason expected a lot from himself. After all, he had all the advantages, including an in-house advisory panel—how could he fail? But he did. Not bigtime, nothing horrible: he didn't flunk any courses, didn't get anyone pregnant or run amok in a convent—nothing like that. He just wasn't doing all that great. He wasn't nearly as successful as his brother and sister were at this age. That bothered Jason, it bothered him a lot. A lot more than anyone knew. He covered up his concern with smiles and jokes, beers and parties, a joint after school which led to tokes between classes which led him to miss classes then whole days!

Then his dealer 'friend' laid some coke on him. O' Wow, how good he felt. It covered up his worries like booze only faster—made everything just fine ... until he ran out.

Replenishing his supply proved expensive for a 16-year-old. So Jason sold his expensive mountain bike (it was a present!). That bought him enough cocaine to last for... ever.

When that ran out, Jason was frantic—hyper—which probably contributed to the accident. It was his dad's car. Expensivo. Father was out of town, fortunately (or unfortunately considering how things turned out). His mother 'lent' him the money to fix the fender. Jason spent the money on a different kind of 'fix.'

The last time his friends saw Jason was after school (they hadn't seen him during school for days). They remember he was in a bad way, strung-out from a three-day bout with cocaine. But still smiling, still joking ... everything was still okay; all he needed was sleep, he said.

Jason went home, lay down with a shotgun and slept forever.

What might have been

All that happened a few years ago. Had Jason slept alone, woke up and faced his parent's shock and disappointment, the brotherly lectures and the sisterly 'looks'—he would have been able to turn his life around. He would have discovered he had what it takes after all. He would be in his middle twenties now. Out of college, into a career, no longer feeling inferior to his siblings, married maybe, returning home for reunions and hanging out with old high school friends remembering the good ol' days.

Maybe next time, Jason...

For those of you reading this—leave your self a 'next time,' however painful the present time may be. When it gets real bad; when life is a misery that keeps getting worse, and all you can think of is escape— hang in there, hang on for dear life. One Jason is one too many.

Knowing how these tragedies happen might help stop them from happening.

No pain is the same

Everyone hurts differently, for different reasons. When there's physical pain combined with mental pain—like Jason's—you are particularly vulnerable. Your mind runs out of control; you don't even want to control it preferring to feed the fires that are burning your insides. At that point, you can't help your self—you're your own worst enemy. Hopefully some-one will be there to lead you out of harm's way. For God's sake open up. Talk before you act. Maybe that's not being 'cool,' but you're 'way beyond that anyway. To quench the flames that are eating you, you've got ring the Fire Alarm.

Success comes easy for the successful. Contrari-wise, once you start a downward spiral, it's hard to pull out, and so easy to just let your self go

> down
>> down
>>> down until you're

so far down in the dumps no one can reach you. So you've got to catch your self before you reach the bottom.

Change the scenery

People who get down on themselves spend too much time alone with themselves. That creates a empty space in which negatives grow like weeds. It's even worse to hang out with a bunch of downers, kids with the same complaints. They'll only reinforce your depressed, negative state of mind. If you can't involve your self with a happy, confident, active crowd—strangers will do. Just get out, expose your self to someplace new. Take a bus to wherever it goes. Surround your self with people, upbeat music. Find something to laugh about. Attend a sporting event.

Best of all—run, run, and run some more. Don't ask why. Just do it. When your body is running, your mind isn't.

All this is designed to occupy your mind. When it's unoccupied it'll turn on you every time. Whose mind is it, anyway? It's there to take orders from your consciousness.

Let's hope you never go near the edge, yet a friend of yours may. They may not confide in you. So many times someone seemed to be acting normally, then the next thing you hear they did this crazy thing. If you had only known…

Most suicides can be stopped. Especially teenage suicides. They're not beyond reach if you reach them in time. They're probably teetering, going though a "Should I or shouldn't I?" argument with themselves. Their doubt is your ally.

Give life a chance

They are one step from eternity. That's no time or place to argue with them. Agree, sympathize—whatever it takes to give life a chance. Just a day. Beg them to stand the pain just one more day to make sure they still feel the same way tomorrow.

None of this deals with their reasons.* It's emergency first-aid. Aid first; remedies come later.

● ●

* They seldom are dissuaded by reason. Suicide contradicts all reason. No other creature knowingly self-destructs. It's against nature, unnatural. It makes no sense so you can't treat it sensibly. To be capable of suicide, to override
continued on next page…

Remember, life is full of agonies and ecstasies; ups and downs. When you're down; it'll seem like you'll never ever be up again. And when a teenager is down, it may be for the first time. So it will be the furthest down you've even been And you'll think you'll be there forever. Because you haven't experienced the way life turns around. That breeds hopelessness that soon turns to helplessness.

Change is your ally

There are going to be so many changes in your life; so many up and downs and turnarounds. Insurmountable problems will be surmounted. Unbearable pain will be borne. Someone with nothing to live for soon will have something to live for! It happens all the time. Two recent examples:

A 30-year-old South American labor leader is thrown into a dungeon and tortured. Day after day, year after year he wanted to die but couldn't. Ten years later he's living in San Francisco, healthy, wealthy, a loving family around him—his captors punished.

A Laotian tribesman loyal to the U.S. during the Vietnam war is captured by the Viet Cong. His fam-

• •

Nature's life preservation instincts, a person must necessarily be insane (from pain, grief, despondency, shame, whatever). Oftentimes suicide is a vindictive act—a way of paying-back those blamed for the pain: parents, an unrequited love or just some faceless 'they' or 'them.' "They'll be sorry..." "I'll show them," "They made me ..." That's why all who jump off the Golden Gate Bridge choose the side facing land—where 'they' live.

ily is murdered. He's tortured, mutilated, starved, and spends years penned-up in a 5' X 5' bamboo cage. Finally he escapes, swims to a fishing boat, wakes up in friendly territory and eventually makes it to the U.S. where he is now the successful owner of a chain of car washes.

Life is full of these turnarounds. Your reprieve may be in the mail.

To end one's life is to play God. You are passing judgement on future events you have no way of fore-telling. Never give up.

Notes to My Self

Notes to My Self

Notes to My Self

15

YOU
ARE NOT
ALONE

"You are home. You belong in the Universe."
—Alan Watts

This is going to another one of those hard-to-swallow chapters. The idea expressed is so simple, so basic to all else, but so contrary to appearances you may wish to switch to a Comic Book. We must risk that because to stop short of what follows would be like not dropping the other shoe. All would be incomplete without this 'secret' of the Universe.

Ready?

Because your consciousness is presently contained in its own separate physical envelope, you get the idea that 'I' am not 'you' anymore than 'you' are a tree. Consequently, each of us feels separate or apart from everyone else. Everything we experience reinforces this illusion of separatness. The tree is not you so it's okay to chop it down. She is not you so it's okay to hurt her. 'They' are not you so its okay to hate 'them.'

Apart from or a part of ?

All the ungood feelings people feel, especially teenage people —shyness, inferiority, suspicion, distrust, jealousy, all that stuff— are fostered by this sense of being apart, all alone in a vast, alien universe. It's little ol' you against all else. No wonder you feel inadequate, oppressed, threatened, scared, confused. No wonder you want to 'drop-out,' run and hide.

But… the 'you' that appears to be separate and at war with every other object is your physical envelope, the ego you.

Hardware contains software

If our essence or consciousness wasn't contained in that outer envelope, that package of flesh that takes up space and casts a shadow, your ego couldn't/ wouldn't exist. It would have no home, nothing to 'puff up.' The ego-you that you take to be all of you is a charade, a shield, as well as a container… the hardware that contains the software. It is the part of you that is diminished when you lose a limb or some organ. From this point of view, the soldier who comes back from the wars in a wheelchair is only 'half a man.' But all he's lost are pieces of his physical facade. If he thinks that's all he is, he feels unwhole: his ego has suffered a loss. But his consciousness—his 'I Am'ness—

is still whole… always was and always will be indivisible, indestructible, which is to say, immortal.

Actually, everything except ego is immortal. Even physical things like rocks and fingers. But the immortality of physical things involves transformations. Bodies, like trees,die and their material is recycled. Bodies are matter and matter is energy. Energy just transforms itself into new forms. A leaf drops to the ground, becomes humus providing energy for new growth. All material forms of energy keep transforming, or regenerating. Pure consciousness (a much higher form of energy) remains constant.

Whether or not you agree with or understand any of the foregoing— make a leap of faith and accept the concept for the sake of discussion. Now we can take the next step forward.

If you are not what you have thought you were —i.e., a separate body/ego apart and distinct from all the other bodies/egos— you must be a part of the whole: *all is one and one is all.* You are everything. And every part of 'everything' must be interdependent. We are all part of a universal ecology.

As a great Hasidic rabbi put it, "If I am I because you are you, and if you are you because I am I, then I am not I and you are not you."

Light bulbs burn out but electricity flows on.
It's as if our bodies were light bulbs. When we are plugged into electrical energy we light up. We ap-

pear to glow independently of each other (albeit some brighter, some dimmer, some red, yellow, white, etcetera). What's interesting about a light bulb is not the bulb but the energy the bulb transforms into light. Bulbs burn out, but the energy flows on to be utilized by other bulbs. Cosmic consciousness is represented by that energy flow. It's always there. It's all there is. That's it.

Conclusion: What we see/experience is a lot of separate bodies (individual light bulbs) plugged into the universal energy source. Because we don't see the connection—there is no see-able cord—we assume we are self-contained light sources with a certain life expectancy.

We do not know what got us to glowing or why, and we exist in constant fear our light will go out. What we need to realize is the bulb, our body, while a wondrous device, is merely the medium, a receptacle; the means of manifesting or expressing consciousness on the physical, Reality I level. Because this medium/body is material, it suffers inevitable wear and tear, deteriorates and finally ceases to function, dies and becomes 'dust.' Just as that burnt-out bulb in our example becomes crumbled glass and oxidizing metal. Seeing this, other bodies/bulbs (who think all they are are bodies/bulbs) believe that's the end: the light went out, it's all over. While the physical reality isn't in fact 'over' but is merely being transformed into other forms of matter, the conscious element—the light source—is unaffected by the body's/bulb's fate. It's just that we can't *see* consciousness anymore than we can see electrical energy before it actualizes a light bulb, and we can't see where it went after it no longer had a bulb to light. Because the consciousness cannot 'see' itself, anymore than you can see the back of your eyes, it's easy to be tricked into this illusion of separateness.

One is all and all is one

What does all this mean to a 16-year-old who's wallowing in a world of separate bodies and conflicting egos? The simple, sensational message is that *you are not an independent object playing a brief and insignificant role in an indifferent universe. You are not in competition with or opposed by other objects (including people) or forces. We are all plugged into the same universal energy source; that which created and forms all objects.* What animates your form (makes it 'glow') is what makes rocks hard and suns shine.* So to dislike or do harm to other objects— including people—is to dislike and harm your self (even though you may be unable to understand the harm done). That's what makes racism so stupid. Instead of treating others as separate lighted bulbs (of different colors), you should remember we are all connected to the same power source.

• •

*We humans are composed of Heavenly material: the atomic elements formed at the universe's birth, the 'Big Bang,' became stars, planets... and people!

143

But… you/he/her/them/they/us/we still have to deal with a world of appearances where bodies are separate and unequal and appear to operate in opposition to one another. How to handle this world of winning and losing without denying the ultimate reality that *one is all and all is one?* The only way to handle both realities—to work both sides of the street—is to consider life as a game.

Life is best lived in the spirit of play. To be sure, it's a game in which you can suffer grievous pain, where cars run over people, where cancers prey and cutthroats prowl. So you must pay attention to the players and the rules. By realizing life's a game composed of egos and objects, you detach your consciousness from it, so you can witness your self playing the game, The game of life gets out of control when you become so immersed in the game that your consciousness can't or won't stand aside to witness what's happening. It's like going to a horror movie and becoming so involved with what's happening on the screen you forget you're in the audience witnessing the spectacle. As a result, you suffer the tortures of the damned. But ain't it nice when the lights come on. What a relief.

As long as you remain conscious of your conscious you, you can retreat from the ego-game—if only long enough to regain your perspective and reenter the contest a better player. Just like going in and out of a movie theater.

Honor your opponents

Another good thing about living life as a game—it makes you appreciate the role of the opposition. You can't have a game without winning and losing, without penalties and rewards. Opponents are an indispensable element of any game. The game of life necessarily involves other people. You know you are winning or losing, good or bad, big or small only in relation to the other players. How you are doing is linked with how others are doing. Realizing that, you can better practice what Jesus preached about loving your enemies. This does not mean you should pretend they are not enemies. Love them *as* enemies... because without a 'bad guy' how could you play 'good guy?'So even in the hard-edged physical world, all things are interdependent.

One last flash about playing life as a game: this recognition keeps conflicts within bounds. Games have rules that players must agree-to. Once you recognize you are a player you can lighten up. Without that recognition there could be no such thing as chivalry, the spirit that keeps warfare within limits. (This spirit is embodied in the Knights Of Olde and warriors of more recent vintage:World War I pilots dueling in the sky would not press the trigger when their opponents ran out of ammo!). If the warring parties lacked chivalry there'd be no stopping total obliteration, wiping out all the players and any more games!

People who become totally attached to the game they are playing will stop at nothing to win. They'll sacrifice their lives and everyone else's—even blow up the whole world. These are extremely dangerous folk, fanatics of one sort or another (usually driven by religious belief). They are the ones who would push the Doomsday button. They must be played with very carefully.

Win some, lose some

In conclusion, play hard, play fair and remain aware that you are playing. That's all you need do. Just stay aware. That way you can't lose even if you don't win. There will be other games, with other outcomes.

Most important, the other players are extensions of your self and should be treated accordingly.

Notes to My Self

Notes to My Self

16

ENJOY
NOW

*Nothing satisfies a person
incapable of enJOYment*

There is too little joy in being young. The reason there is so little joy in it is because the people who run the world, the old(er) people, are a product of a goal-obsessed culture. So youth is no end unto itself but a preparatory period when one gets ready for adulthood... or so they'd have you think, and act.

It has been said, "Man is the only creature who doesn't know the chief business of life is to enjoy it." Indeed, if life isn't fun, what's it supposed to be? A pain?

As a species, we suffer from *pleasure anxiety*. That is, we hesitate to enjoy ourselves out of fear something bad will follow. In other words, "it may rain on my parade so I won't march." Having fun makes us feel guilty. Perhaps it is a hangover from the concept of original sin.

Whatever the reason, there's too little joy in Teensville (where the capacity is greatest!). Pleasure-seeking for its own sake definitely is not the way to get ahead in the grown-up world. Here we refer to pointless pleasures: the joy of singing on a crowded bus; chasing a butterfly, catching a wave or flying a kite.

Second-class status

Because adulthood seems to be the objective of youth, being young is somehow less desirable, a lower order of existence, a second-class class. Young people are put-down when they act youthful, and lauded when they act grown-up. The way for teenagers to win the respect of adults is to become goal-oriented: to begin leafing through medical manuals or studying the stock market. Peter Pans are an object of concern.

Always striving, never arriving

Yet the truth is: unless one is able to live fully in the present, the future is a hoax. There is no point whatever in making plans for a future you'll never be able to enjoy. And the future adults would have you plan for may make you rich, but not joyful. For when those plans mature, you'll find your self planning for some other future beyond. You'll never be able to sit back and say, "I've arrived! I'm where I want to be. Now I can start chasing rainbows." Successful people are seldom seen resting on their laurels. The rich keep getting richer because they dare not stop making money. They may kid themselves that the pursuit gives them pleasure, but what it gives them is power. Pursuing goals that can never be reached is no pleasure.

Our educational system—designed by adults—can be thanked for substituting achievement for pleasure. It prepares us for an illusive future instead of helping us to enjoy NOW; to be alive NOW. We are conditioned by a system arranged in grades or steps, each leading to more steps. But that stairway never ends until death. (And then we face that big stairway in the sky—the one leading to Heaven!)

Joy is good for you

Joy is not an anti-social force. It is not the exclusive reserve of immature children or a refuge for self-indulgent, freeloading hippies. Joy is a beneficial state of mind; a healthy state of being: joyful people are demonstrably healthier than sourpusses. And have you ever known a joy-filled person (if, indeed, you know one) who is likely to start a war, commit a murder, beat their spouse, abuse their children, have a nervous breakdown or bear a grudge? Joyful people are a pleasure to be around. They spread joy. People like that should be celebrated. Every nation should appoint a Minister Of Joy, responsible for of Holidays, festivals and celebrations.

It's one thing to urge you to enjoy now. It's another thing to do it—without leaving the mainstream of our culture. The trick is how to deal with the materialism that surrounds you and still enJOY. Keeping the discussion on that material, Reality I level, the way to do it is *find a ladder that's fun to climb*. Even if you never reach the top, or find another ladder waiting there, you may count your self fortunate. Next question: how to pick the right ladder? That's the stuff of the following chapter...

Notes to My Self

Notes to My Self

17

FOLLOW
YOUR BLISS

*Choose a job you love and
you'll never have to work a day in your life.*
—Confucius

For those of you who don't make a career of being a student—good work if you can get it—earning a living is what you will do (un)happily ever after leaving school.

Most men die in the saddle, and most women with a mop in hand, women's lib notwithstanding.

But between now and when working for a living becomes unavoidable, there's the question of schooling. As you may have noticed, education and achievement go hand-in-glove in our capitalistic culture. Nowadays, un(der)educated, self-made men/women are as rare as Ferraris in Patagonia. The folks who captain our industries almost always have a MBA. And the people who educate our moguls are required to have a Ph.D after their names. It goes without saying that Professions and higher learning go hand-in-hand.

Today, a Bachelors degree is what a High School diploma was yesterday.

Learning by doing

Not that a college education qualifies you for the real world of business. The marketplace remains the best place to learn the ways of the marketplace. Four years in the Marketing Department of Proctor & Gamble will make you a better marketing person than the same amount of time working with University models. Trouble is—you won't get into P&G's Marketing Department without a BA, probably an MBA. The reason is (though P&G would never admit it), there are so many BAs sitting in every waiting room that companies always have a misery of choice. All else being equal, they figure the better educated person is a safer bet.

This overabundance of degree people is growing exponentially. Soon, close to 40% of everyone between 20 and 30 will have a college degree, many with masters and doctorates. Considering this competition, it'll be difficult to launch your self into the executive echelons without collegiate credentials.*

● ●

---

* Were this not the case, there would be much to recommend using your educational funds to finance a world tour; travel being a better 'finishing school' than a college campus.

Blue collars and no collars

There are, however, other worlds beyond business, the sciences and humanities. There are plumbers, tool-and-dye makers, owners of hardware stores, lumberjacks and teamsters, first mates, vocalists, ski instructors, garbage men, tillers of the soil, disc jockeys and horse jockeys, writers, nurserymen, steeplejacks, sign painters, clerks and clerics, warehousemen, dancers, bicycle messengers, burgermeisters, musicians, clowns, hardrock miners, waiters, forest rangers, bus drivers, &c. Plus all those people involved in 'high technology,' specifically 'electronics,' which includes computer sciences and telecommunications. What plastics was to the 1950s, electronics is today— a mind-boggling field of opportunity.*

Many of the jobs listed above do not require a higher education. And many of these open-to-anyone jobs will prove more rewarding, moneywise and otherwise. Matter of fact, with everyone vying for white collar jobs, you may find blue collar work offers the most choice.

Speaking of choice, when in doubt about a career/job, take the advice of Joseph Campbell, educa-

• •

* While this field will employ 50-million people in the U.S., billions of people will employ their handiwork: computer-based technology. Those who grow up computer-illiterate will form a new economic underclass. Do not join their ranks! If you use school for nothing else, use it to master the computer. Because if that electronic lash-up is a mystery when you graduate, you'll enter the workforce with two strikes against you.

tor *extrodinaire*, who said, "Follow your bliss," meaning: do what you want to do. Because when you like doing something, you'll do it well. Do it even if it isn't monetarily rewarding. Because personal satisfaction is worth more than gold, and never loses it value.

What's your Swadharma?

Hindu philosophy says each individual has his or her *swadharma*, which means one's individual law of development. Determining what yours is means assessing a number of factors. First is heredity: what you have received from your ancestors. You did not spring out of nothing; you inherited certain talents and tendencies. Then there is environment: the socio-economic, political, educational, cultural and climatic conditions under which you were reared. All these and more determine your *swadharma*. If you are compelled or persuaded to work at something contrary to your *swadharma* you will find success and enjoyment difficult.

Over and above the question of *swadharma*, do not readily accept meaningless, dehumanizing, repetitive tasks, nor those that blatantly exploit the weaknesses of others. There's no satisfaction much less enjoyment in such work, and forty or fifty years is a helluva long time to stay dissatisfied. Don't even do it for a short time because before you know it, you'll have accumulated real or imagined reasons for not being able to change course. Ruts deepen quickly. When deep enough, you can't see your way out, or what you're missing.

This is terribly important: Find employment that isn't methodical, that doesn't rot your abilities, kill your spirit or compromise your principles. Because the only way to bear such a job is to live in the future; that is, stop living in the present in the hope of future advancement, financial reward and retirement. Never sacrifice the present. It is the only thing you can count on. NOW is all there is to life.

Money is more-ish

When money becomes the sole object, the goal, the reason to choose one job over another—you've just bought yourself a one-way ticket to Nowheresville. Not because money is inherently 'evil' (it's not—it's a most convenient medium of exchange). But money makes a lousy goal. Goals should be attainable. But nobody has ever gained enough money. Money is a more-ish commodity: the more you want the more you get the more you need the more you want, etc. Very frustrating. It's a carrot you can never get your teeth into.

It's been written, "He who wants money does not really know what he wants... his desires are limitless, and no one can tell how to deal with him." When your aim in life is something less illusive—like winning the Indianapolis 500 or becoming a Talk Show host—you have the right kind of goal. When you pursue tangible objectives that involve your desires, you will enjoy the effort of getting there, whether or not you ever do get there. Destinations once reached often prove disappointing. If you didn't enjoy the trip en route, then it will have been a total waste. Remember—all you can really count on is *now.* If you aren't enjoying *now*, you lose.

On the subject of 'goals,' it should be acknowledged that there are tactical, short-range goals, and strategic or long-range goals. Strategic goals concern values or principles—the stuff that determine what manner of person you are which, in turn, determines the approach you take to reach your tactical goals. Many, if not most people, are not conscious of having a strategic, lifelong goal. "To be happy" is the usual reply. But "being happy" is an effect; the result of being something else (like tolerant and compassionate).

Beggars can't be choosers
Returning to the question of avoiding uninvolving work—it should be conceded that in times of a deep economic recession, it's not always possible to be choosey. Digging ditches is preferable to standing in line for hand-outs (if only because our society honors workers, while it makes nonworkers pay for their welfare benefits by forfeiting their dignity). So, if and when you are stuck with a nothing job, apply the principle of detachment by witnessing your self digging the ditch. Digging is just what's happening to

the physical/ego you. Your body is doing the digging while the conscious you observes. Maybe you can't dig that scene, but it's the way to bear anything unpleasant.

Most often though, there is work available that involves the conscious you versus drudgery which lets the mind wander, and it usually wanders to feelings of self-pity, regret and resentment. The world is full of opportunity if you but seek it out. If you want to write, become a Forest Service fire lookout, leaving you the time and isolation to focus on writing. If you like the sun, get a Lifeguard's certificate. If you like the sea, ship out. *Do what you like.* That's the best possible career advice. If you don't like what you do, you won't do it well and will not be rewarded. Square pegs find round holes difficult to penetrate and withdraw from.

Be Creative

It should also be mentioned, there are basically two kinds of work. One kind creates or initiates— starts others in motion; makes things happen. Builders are one example. The second kind reacts to the first kind, like a carpenter reacts to the builder. The builder decides to create a house, which provides the carpenter/plumber/backhoe operator, et al. with employment. The advertising man reacts to the needs of advertisers, like a stock broker reacts to the needs of investors. Because initiators usually have more to lose, they also are in a position to gain the most. The fastest growing employment segment is the so-called 'service industry,' that serves (reacts) to the needs of others. But what the world needs more of is initiators, the enablers, risk-takers. They are the creators, creating the needs others fill.

Whatever you do, do it well. Give it your best. Old-fashioned advice, but sound. When any job is done poorly, you lose two ways: 1) you lose your self-respect, and 2) you lose any chance to grow. Quality always seeks its proper level.

Notes to My Self

Notes to My Self

18

GIVE ALL YOU'VE GOT

Half-hearted efforts are returned in kind

Most of society's sins are committed in a misguided effort to help people avoid failure. For example: In most of the world's industrialized countries it's pretty hard to starve to death. And in the U.S., at least, it's even harder to fail at (public) school. The harder the system works to ensure everyone will eat and be educated and receive equal opportunities, the lower our standards become. A sad commentary considering the good intentions involved. But the results speak for themselves.

Loafers receive half a loaf

People need to take risks; to 'put the peddle to the metal.' It's what keeps our internal machinery running smoothly—prevents carbon buildup. When a high-revving engine is allowed to loaf along mile after mile, it's going to develop problems—it wasn't designed to operate like that! But that's what the public educational system does to you; that's what the corporate management system is doing to your parents. As things now stand, it's virtually impossible to fail in school. You can be caught fiddling with a live hand grenade in math class, and after 'suffering' a reprimand in the principal's office and promising never to do it again, you'll be back in line for a diploma. This everyone-makes-it system produces a great middling mass of mediocrity—a nation of half-educated people. But that's not the worst of it.

When kids don't have a proving ground that really tests their mettle, they are going to invent their own challenges, and these usually take antisocial forms: driving like maniacs, vandalism, gang wars and other forms of thrill-seeking. Russian Roulette is what bored, cooped-up people play.

Put your self to the test

Athletics provide a trial-by-fire ordeal, especially competitive mano-y-mano sports like boxing and track & field events. The safer society makes living, the more necessary are such physical 'tests.' Now that we have no more continents to discover or new oceans to chart, we turn to such esoteric activities as paddling across the Atlantic in a bathtub or climbing Mt. Everest blindfolded.

Trouble is—most young people (most everybody!) don't know what they're missing. Face it: few teenagers want school to be tougher so that 'A's are rare as hen's teeth and failures are held back or kicked out. You don't realize that the reason you smartass the teacher or disrespect any authority is to take a risk, to test limits.

All this recommends you develop positive ways to test your worth and establish your limits. Commit your self to something, anything that involves risking failure—whether it's learning the guitar or pole-vaulting. Whatever it is, it should involve a sacrifice, giving-up something, or else attainment isn't so sweet. An Olympic-bound swimmer swims laps morning, noon and night, week in and week out, while his/her friends are just hangin' out. When you give-up all those movies and cokes and dates, you're damn well going to make all the effort pay-off. That's what commitment is all about. It starts with a decision, as opposed to just floating along with the tide and dipping a toe in life.

A commitment is essentially an agreement or contract you make with your self. That's the only kind of commitment that matters. (Sometimes it helps to 'advertise' your commitment to the outside world—to let them know what you've decided to accomplish. That helps you remain firm in your resolve.) This doesn't include things you're supposed/expected to do, like get good grades or mow the lawn. We're talking about things you don't *have to do,* like becoming skateboard champ or the Captain of the Debating Team or starting a small business on the side.

When you commit your self to a course of action that tests your mental and/or physical perseverance, and you hold true to that goal—you're going to come out a head taller. Even if you don't become a champion or the best at something... so long as *you* know you gave it your best, you'll be a winner. There is nothing to equal the sense of worth this produces. It is a satisfaction that is all too rare these days.

Could of, might of...

Practically everybody holds back a little something to protect their ego. If they fail, they can always say, "Well, I could have been the best had I *really* tried." How many times can you truthfully say you put-out 100%; gave it everything you had? When you only give 80%, you'll only get an 80% return. Until you go all-out, you'll never know complete satisfaction, or success. Giving 100% is the basis of self-esteem. People don't even love each other 100% out of fear of being hurt. You'll never be loved 100% until you love in the same fashion. Holding back is just cheating your self. If you're going to stand in front of a microphone and sing—then for God's sake SING ... let go absolutely. Don't try to protect your self by holding anything back. Even if 'winning' is all that counts with you, when you give 100% and you don't get a standing ovation, at least you know where you stand. (Most people never find that out!)

No more 'maybes'
People who only go halfway are always bothered with 'maybes.' "Maybe I could have been great had I really tried." Well, if you really tried and you weren't great, then you'd know your limitations. There's value in that. Limits are only troublesome when you don't know what they are, so you aim too low or seek something that's beyond the reach of your talent or physical abilities. But you'll never know if you don't put your talents/capabilities to the test. And the only fair test is one that stretches you.

Some limits are easier to establish than others, of course. If you're into weight lifting, it's easy to determine what weight is beyond your ability to press. Most physical tests fall into that black-and-white category. It's the talent area that's more difficult to assess. This is where most people hold-back. This is where it's tougher to let your self go… to go for broke! But no performer ever attained greatness without giving 100%* (which explains why there are so few great performers.) Great talent is not rare. The world is full of talented people who *could be* great but won't be because they don't give 100%. The

• •

* To manage that, singers, actors, comics, dancers leave their off-stage self backstage in order to 'get into' the character/music on-stage.

person who makes the most of a little talent is more to be admired than the person who made little of a lot of talent.

Unrealized potential is such a waste. It's like wasting natural resources. And no matter how the possessors of that talent may rationalize this waste, it eats away at their self-confidence. Having talent is therefore something of a burden. You are obliged to utilize it; make the most of it. And 'the most' equals 100%.

To recap: Our society tries to insulate people against failure by accepting half-hearted efforts. This leaves most of us untested and untried, which generates a lack of self-esteem. So we turn to things like clothes and cars and tagging to prop-up our self-image.

But the only meaningful achievement is personal: something you've done that's as good as you can possibly do ... after much trial and error. You don't need money for that. You don't need understanding parents or a good neighborhood. All you need is your self; a willingness to commit your self and do something as well as you can do it. When you've done that, you've done all you can do. Win or lose—you'll be way ahead.

Notes to My Self

19

WAKE
UP

A New Age is dawning

The new millennium cometh: three zeros are about to appear on *Homo sapiens'* odometer. With the changeover will come a receptivity and tolerance for new ideas, new approaches, a fresh start, turning a new leaf—what social commentators are wont to call "new paradigms."

There is no special 'magic' in a calendar event. The number '2000' has no more meaning than any other number before or after it. Numbers, like clocks, are just man-made measures, established for our own convenience. Nevertheless, ushering in a new millennium does have an effect on the public consciousness that can and should have far-reaching consequences, all of them potentially positive.

An all-time first

The last time the world celebrated a new millennium mankind was grovelling in the Dark Ages. People were too burdened with misery to celebrate. So the upcoming event marks the first time in human history that we will really experience such an occasion.

Until now, a new century was a big deal. Even these 100-year milestones marked turning points in mankind's progress. The expression "New Age" was popularized in 1900 (the beginning of the 20th Century) to mark the Western World's new-found interest in Eastern spiritual traditions. As Buddhism, Taoism, Hinduism, etc. were integrated into the Christian culture they produced hybrids that became known as "New Age" congregations. The more enlightened or higher-minded of these, Unity and Science Of Mind (to name two), prefer to be identified as "New Thought" perhaps to separate themselves from the more kooky and cultish spin-offs. Be that as it may, "New Age" is not new. But it continues to identify seekers who, while not abandoning Christian traditions, are finding their spiritual home includes planks imported from India, Tibet and China.

The Age of Acquarius previewed

Whatever the reason, however it has happened, there appears to be a great upwelling of spirituality taking place here, there and everywhere. Mankind's spiritual nature is gaining sway over our brute side. Consider how far we've come in the last 500 years, much less 5000 years. Can you imagine a pack of Vikings rallying to halt the slaughter of seal pups, or a bunch of Elizabethans protesting the cutting down of giant sequoia, or ancient Romans rising up in righteous indignation over an unjust war?

What a difference a millennium makes

It is interesting to chart man's progress from our lumbering ancestors to our present elegance. Ten centuries ago the great mass of humanity lived as peasants and slaves. It required dawn-to-dusk labor to half-fill their stomachs. Survival left no time or desire to develop a vision of a higher order of existence. After the Renaissance lifted our eyes and the Industrial Revolution eliminated the Feudal System, mankind moved closer to its potential.

This evolution from a bent-over beast to *Homo sapiens'* present status is testimony that man, like Rome, wasn't built in a day ... or even six days. With every generation we become more refined: closer to the angels and further from the animals. And seeing as how your generation is next in line to take charge of this progress, it is important to know you are on the cusp of what promises to be a great leap forward (if we don't slip and nuke ourselves back into the Stone Age in the meantime). So a few more words about our past as a prelude to the future would seem in order.

Blue is new

Did you know that just 5,000 years ago (a mere tick on the evolutionary clock) civilized, sophisticated Greeks, Persians, Chinese, et al. could not recognize the color blue? It's true. Aristotle spoke of the "tri-colored rainbow," Homer of the "wine-dark sea." In the bible, the Rig-Veda, Herodotus' histories, along with the epic *Iliad & Oddessy*, the sky is described thousands of times without one mention of 'blue.' That's because the eye's ability to differentiate the full spectrum of color is relatively recent.

Unless you are an anthropologist, this is no big thing—except that it demonstrates that (wo)man is developing, being perfected.

What *is* important for you to know is not all of us are being perfected at the same rate. Somebody had to see 'blue' before somebody else. Blueness didn't just happen to everyone simultaneously—as if God declared blue to exist and splashed it across the sky one morning so everyone could look up and exclaim "Hallelujah, it's blue." Because only a few could see blue before the many, early blue see-ers surely had trouble relating what they saw to their blue-blind friends. (Maybe the first loony bins were filled with folk who babbled about blue.)

Immorality is better than no morality
Morality, without which the Golden Rule will never rule, appears to be mankind's latest acquisition. Being a relatively new trait, there are many people with no morality* and many more who are only partially moral, on a conditional, now-and-then basis.

A working description of "morality" would be someone with a well-developed conscience—sense of right and wrong—who instinctively feels what another person is feeling, hence is likely to treat others in the same manner he/she would like to be treated ("Do unto others ..."). Trouble happens when the moral person assumes everyone else is also moral. At this point in man's development that is not a fair assumption. You will find your self playing with people who do not play by your (moral) rules. This can be awfully confusing and occasionally dangerous.

It is almost impossible for a compassionate/moral person to conceive how someone with the same physical attributes can coolly torture another human being or commit other overt acts of premeditated cruelty to their own kind (much less dumb animals). Anyone who could casually stick red hot pins in some poor wretch's eyeballs is *not* like you; he/she only looks

• •

* Being without morals is being amoral. Immorality is acting contrary to what you know is right. Therefore only moral people can be said to be immoral.

177

like you. That person lacks compassion: the ability to put their self in the other person's shoes; to feel what they are feeling. So a moral person is easy prey for amoral people. And it is quite impossible to judge who is playing by which rules, Many amoral people regularly attend church and mouth pious platitudes. (After all, they don't know they are amoral!). But when the going gets tough they'll show their true colors: lying, cheating, even killing to help themselves.

Presuming you can be counted among the moral majority, you will be shocked and surprised when someone proves to be lacking morality. At least now you know why some people can be sooo bad.

All the above bears testimony that the so-called Age of Aquarius (roughly akin to Heaven on Earth) is a-comin'. It will not be long before all men and women possess a moral sense; when humankind is incapable of doing unto others what we would not have done unto us. Fast on the heels of that evolutionary plateau will come the ultimate faculty: Cosmic Consciousness, an innate sense of inter-connectedness. Some few individuals possess this now—about as many as could see 'blue' in Homer's time. What one has, all will have. Today's exceptions will be tomorrow's rule. It is inevitable—just a matter of time.

Notes to My Self

20

THE FUTURE IS NOT WHAT IT USED TO BE

A preview of coming attractions

You just finished reading about the "New Age" that's dawning. But don't let that lull you into thinking this awakening is an automatic, can't-miss sure-thing.

We may be on the threshold of the so-called Aquarian Age, but that threshold has two doors facing it. One opening leads to something approximating Heaven On Earth. The other way opens to Doomsday. Which is which?

Coming soon: The Moment of Truth

You and your friends will be the ones who decide. If it's excitement you want—being involved in momentous events—you couldn't have picked a better time to grow up. This is the first time in human history we've had the means of destroying ourselves along with our terrestrial habitat. And at the same time we've never been so close to elevating ourselves above the animal kingdom into the spiritual realm.

All the chips will be on the table when it's your turn to step up to the plate. Every hope that ever has been hoped, every prayer that ever has been sent Heavenward, every pain that ever has been endured, every lesson ever learned, every battle ever won or lost, every lesson ever learned, every poem ever penned, every kind word ever spoken throughout human history—*all this* will be made meaningless or meaningful by the actions taken or not taken by your generation. (If it's responsibility you want—you'll get all you can handle, and then some!)

We've lived with the threat of nuclear destruction hanging over our heads for some time now. That won't go away as long as these weapons remain stockpiled. Less dramatic but no less horrendous consequences loom on the environmental front during your tour of duty.

Lookout above and below

The destruction of the ozone layer won't snuff the human race in an instant! But unless the thinning of this layer of atmosphere that protects our hide from the sun's ultraviolet rays ceases instanter, you'd better start digging yourself a hole and learn to like living underground.

Then there is the much ballyhooed, "Greenhouse" effect whereby the polar ice caps melt to change the face of our globe socially, politically, economically, and geographically. (When was the last time a new generation faced that kind of challenge?!) Sure, ice caps have melted before. But the causes were natural, as in gradual. Anyway, humans weren't around then to live with the consequences. ("Live" is a poor word choice. "Sink or swim" better describes the consequences.)

There are other Armageddon-size threats you'll be facing—but the purpose of this chapter isn't to make you fearful. Quite the contrary—these global problems contain the seeds of your salvation. Consider…

When everyone's threatened, everyone helps

Until recent times, all mankind's problems were localized. A famine here; pestilence there; a horrible war in one place; terrible tyranny another place. As long as it was only Ethiopians who were starving; or Russians who were oppressed; or Jews who were slaughtered—the problem could be lived with. A perfect example is to be found in the current AIDS plague. As long as it was thought to be a problem unique to homosexuals—it wasn't *our* problem. Now, suddenly, it's crossed the tracks to the straight side of town where it has mainstream population by the throat. Now it's become everyone's problem! What a difference that makes! There's nothing like a common threat to create a common concern to produce a common determination to solve it. (Look up the word 'commonweal.') Apparently that's what it takes to make us realize we are all in this together; it's one for all, or all for naught.

Now that the whole world and all the life forms that inhabit it are threatened equally and simultaneously with extinction, one of two scenarios will take place.

One, we will continue to squabble over whose fault it is, or who should do what about it... until there is no one to left to blame or fight with.

Or, two, we will drop our differences forthwith and join together in a common, global effort to undo what our differences did!

It's a damned shame we have to be pushed to the brink of extinction before recognizing we're all God's children—one vineyard nourishes all. Let us hope the light dawns before we are over the edge and falling. Then it will do no good to cling to the rocks that are falling with us.

● ●

Footnote: Years ago, in the 50s sometime, there was a second-rate SciFi flick with a first-rate plot. With apologies to the its writer whom we can't give due credit for the lack of a remembered title—the story went like this: An advanced alien culture from another solar system sent an emissary to warn our globe's warring nations to make peace among ourselves lest our terrestrial arguments ignite a nuclear war whose backlash would upset the equilibrium of other worlds. Well, of course—you know what happened next: This world's leaders gathered as ordered to hear the Emissary's "Either/Or" ultimatum. As soon as they heard it, each began defending themselves and blaming the others. Thereupon, the inter-planetary messenger issued a Cosmic, "Shut-up", and proceeded to read them the galactic riot act, "Set aside your gratuitous gripes and petty peeves from this moment onward, or you shall all be annihilated without another word of warning." Too bad we can't have Peace On Earth by proclamation. But next best is a high tide that turns the Pentagon into an island.

Notes to myself

21

DO SOMETHING, FOR A CHANGE

When you pray for potatoes pick up a hoe

The last Chapter dumped all the problems that have accumulated over the millennia right in your lap. This isn't the first time an incoming generation has been saddled with the outgoing generation's failures. (Although it may be the last time!) It's almost one of the standard Rites of Passage to have the weight of the world placed on the shoulders of each succeeding generation. ("If once you don't succeed—try, try again.").

The preceding chapter's bottom line was: the problems won't fix themselves ... and if you don't fix them, there'll be no one left to fix them: *we've come to the end of the line and look who's standing there!* Also it was said you are up to the task ... if you all pull together.

A time for heros

There you have it. Your generation either will be Humankind's All-Time Numero Uno HERO, or the generation that presided over *Homo sapiens'* demise. The Doomsday option, it must be said, is easiest to accomplish: All you have to do is *nothing*. The Hero's role will take some doing, including the cooperation of all races, creeds, colors and political persuasions.

Do not allow the enormity of the task to stop you. Epic journeys are completed one step at a time ... starting with the first step. For inspiration, study The Dark Ages. They were no picnic. But look what they led to, The Renaissance. Talk about breakthroughs! It was as if humankind had been held prisoner in the cave of its birth. Only we didn't realize we were imprisoned so there was no escape. Then, all of a sudden, there appeared a pinpoint of light—but in the blackness that was The Dark Ages, it blazed like a beacon. The huddled multitudes rose and staggered towards the illumination—like moths to a bright bulb—and suddenly found themselves outside their cave into a totally new world full of light.

Lead on

So, too, can your generation be the torchbearer that leads your children out of the gully of gloom and guilt—up to a higher level of existence (from which vantage point you will experience dimensions we've been blind to).

According to The Scriptures, The Children Will Lead Us. The wisdom behind that ancient writ was touched on earlier, *"Teenagers are a lot closer to making their lives work than anyone else ... closer by virtue of not having had time to get very far off course."* The adult world will sniff and snort at the very suggestion that you—a bunch of snotty-nosed, self-indulgent kids—could save the world.

A few will become many

Ignore those naysayers (remembering what a mess they've made of things). You can do it: *Write history rather than repeat it.* It's not all that difficult, really. Just remain conscious of that objective; speak of it; act on it. Be the initiator. You will attract converts by example. A few will become many.

Sound the trumpets

To succeed does not require keeping score. There'll be no missing The New Age. Breakthroughs are not slow, gradual turnarounds. Going from medieval darkness to a radiant Renaissance was not an agonizing, inch-at-a-time process, but a sudden, glorious burst of spontaneous energy—a blossoming, announced with blaring trumpets and the applause of millions.

Martin Luther King knew it would happen like that—not miraculously, but by the accumulation of all the right thoughts and actions to-date. Fear and suspicion will disappear, virtually overnight. Our enemies will be revealed as shadows... our own shadows! Who needs weapons then? Who needs walls, borders, threats and coercion? The sun shines on everyone.

The energy that fuels change builds slowly... at first. But your generation has inherited almost a full tank! You have only to add one more drop. So what are you waiting for? *Do something, for a change.*

Apologia

The last couple of chapters is not the sort of stuff that should be included in a manual for teenagers. Asking a teenager to turn away from the mirror, drop his/her books and skip Friday night's party to mount the barricades and defend the world against the forces of evil is asking a lot—probably too much, considering what's already on your plate. Even if you don't answer this call to arms now—for which you are forgiven—there still will be time when "18" rolls around and you have the Right To Vote. Then you *must* answer the call. Nothing could be more important. Jobs, affluence, freedom, love, the quality of your life— life itself—depend on your actions. Action follows thought. So start thinking, in preparation for *doing something, for a change.* If you don't, history will repeat itself... only this time, there'll be no repeat performance. You'll be the last act!

Notes to Myself

MOPPING UP

Bits 'n' pieces too short to call chapters,
too good to throw out

IN PRAISE OF DIVERSITY

There are two ways of looking at life. One way is from several thousand miles out in space. From that perspective there are no nations or borders; no white faces or brown faces; no Catholics or Jews; no Communists or Capitalists; no liberals or conservatives... just a small, round, blue planet floating all by itself in empty space.

From this vantage point it's beyond comprehension that all over that little lonesome globe there are creatures called *Homo sapiens* who, since time immemorial, have been hacking each other to pieces because of their color and their belief systems.

The other way to look at life here on the planet Earth is from your present point of view: up close and personal—where all the hacking and hating takes place.

Even from this viewpoint it remains incomprehensible why the inhabitants of this tiny planet (located in an inconsequential solar system on the fringes of a relatively small galaxy within an incredibly immense Universe) should have reason to hate/resent/distrust each other. One would think we'd be more inclined to hug one another considering our precarious position in the cosmos.

But, no... instead of loving one another; we grow up suspicious of and fighting with our fellows.

How stupid. How pathetic. How unnecessary.

If you stop and analyse why we humans fight/hate/ resent/dislike each other, it is because of differences. Someone who looks different, sounds different, acts different, believes different, lives different than you somehow represents a threat to you. To put it a different way: someone who talks like you, dresses like you; believes like you; lives like you makes you feel more secure.

In some ways, teenagers are the worst offenders. You flock together in such tight little societies that 99% of the rest of the world is excluded. You only feel comfortable in the company of those your own age; who speak the same jargon; who wear the same clothes; who attend the same school; who belong to the same gang; who like the same music; who hang out at the same mall.

Again, this is so stupid. All the pain and unhappiness it causes is totally unnecessary. Perhaps worst of all—you are eliminating all the joys that diversity/ variety provides. It's as if you joined an all-saxophone band. Nothing wrong with saxophones. But they sound a helluva lot better when mixed with brass, string and percussion instruments. (That's what produces harmony, as well as symphonies!)

Think about it—what a sad and boring place this would be if all the birds were blue; all the flowers were red; all the days were sunny.

What's so special about Mother Earth is its bio-diversity. Likewise, what's so marvelous about this nation is its variety: its combination of races, creeds, politics, values, *ad infinitum*. Diversity/variety is what makes us so unique; so interesting; so resourceful and strong.

Instead of wishing everyone was the same as you—be thankful for differences. Likewise, be grateful for symphonic music; for Asian immigrants; for Born-Again Christians; for turnips; for Shakespeare; for fault-finding parents... for all the different ingredients that make-up this wild and spicy stew called life. Celebrate differences. Welcome diversity. In so doing, you not only will make your neighborhood, town, state, nation and planet a better place to live—you will be a happier, healthier human being. Guaranteed.

LIVE AND LET LIVE

Continuing on the same subject as the preceeding piece, the following letter was published on the Editorial Page of the San Francisco CHRONICLE. It is a most persuasive comment in favor of the "I'm okay, you're okay" philosophy. Read and reap:

"Editor—If I were to smoke marijuana in my home, does that harm you? If I wanted to marry another man, how would that hurt you? If I were to read pornography on the Internet, in what way would you be injured? If I want to pay a prostitute for consenual sex, why do you feel a need to not allow it? If I am dying and in pain and want to end my life, what compels you to forcibly stop me?

I have no desire to do any of the above, but I couldn't imagine trying to stop anyone else from doing them. I seem to be missing a gene that makes me want to control other people's lives. What is wrong with me?

I understand people's desires to pass laws that protect themselves from harm. I'm glad it's against the law for you to steal from me to buy drugs. I'm very glad it's against the law for you to force your religion on me, because I know you really want to.

What am I lacking that you have that makes you so fervent in wanting to control my lifestyle even when it doesn't harm you or even involve you? Why do you think the lifestyle you have chosen is better for me than the one I have chosen for me? What compels you to force me to live just like you?

—Kevin Welsh

Some who read this may see it as an argument in favor of what they deem immoral behavior. They should read it a second time.

It is a plea for tolerance; not encouragement to persue any of the examples given.

BEWARE THE CATHODE RAY TUBE

You're tired of hearing about the negative effects television produces on our psyche and society. Because you've grown-up surrounded by the tube, it's hard to see it as a threat or an enemy. TV is a fact of life and there's nothing no one can say that will make it go away. But it might be possible to change your viewing habits—i.e., the quantity if not the quality of what you watch on TV. It's worth a try.

Once upon a time, more than 50 years ago, much the same warnings and worries were attached to movies. It was feared kids spent too much time in Hollywood's Fantasyland, making them unable to cope with the hard-edge world outside the theater. Whatever the merits of those concerns, the threat was diminished by virtue of time, distance and expense. Kids didn't have the wherewithal to see more than one or two movies a week. And because the movie house wasn't in-house, it took time and trouble to see a show. You had to leave home to see a movie. That helped separate fiction from fact! That's the big difference with TV. Now the same 21" screen that delivers news (reality), also delivers fiction. One bleeds into the other, hour after hour; day after day. It's surrounds you like wallpaper.

So there's no going back to those days when people sat around staring at the invisible sounds of radio waves. But there's a lot to be said in favor of moderation. And the easiest way to moderate the amount of time you spend in front of the TV is to avoid programs you don't really care about. Face it— probably half the time you spend watching TV is spent watching stuff you don't particularly care about. Reserve your TV time for the special and important stuff like the World Series, the Olympics; the Academy Awards, as well as your favorite shows. But turn off the dross and the drivel. Surely you've got something better to do.

SPEAK UP

In case you hadn't noticed—teenagers aren't the greatest communicators. O' you do okay when it comes to intramural conversation (between yourselves) which involve non-verbal forms of communication—i.e., lotsa body language. And like all affinity groups, teenagers develop their own secret language (which is unique to each generation, locale and lifestyle*) the purpose of which is to *avoid* communicating with outsiders—e.g., non-teenagers. But when you're standing on the carpet facing a disapproving parent; a disbelieving teacher—officialdom of any sort—you seldom receive a fair hearing. Because what they hear and what you mean/feel don't jibe! Audiences comprised of your elders are intimidating, critical. You are expected to speak *their* language; communicate on *their terms*. They will seldom pause to translate; to interpret your monosyllables and jargon.

That legendary "Generation Gap" is really a communications gap. Adults don't respect what you say because of the way you say it. Most times they don't even hear you! A conversation with your elders too often begin and ends with a statement/edict/proclamation from them. They may appear to be listening

• •

* Blacks have their Ebonics, Jazz musicians have their jive, as do gays, lawyers, New Englanders, admen, conservatives, Communists, medical people, mattress salespeople, et al.

when you respond, but they have decided, more or less unconsciously, to discount your reply. It is O' so rare when anyone from the other side of 30 listens with interest and respect to your views.

This is just one of the many frustrations that come from looking grown-up and acting your age. The only way to change it is to stop acting your age—i.e., *sound* old for your age. There's nothing that impresses the father of your date so much as an earnest youngman who volunteers his concern over this month's record Trade Deficit. Those of you who either can't or won't play that game are inclined to do the opposite: to be unforthcoming; never volunteer anything; act sullen; mumble; focus your eyes downward. That puts an end to those one-way conversations.

No wonder young people prefer their own company. To avoid Know-It-All adults, you close ranks, form tight little inner circles as a way to keep out discordant elements—anyone who doesn't look like you; talk like you, think like you, act like you. That may make you feel secure, but it sure doesn't let you in for new experiences, ideas. Sub cultures are comfortable but stifling; a bunch of closed-minded people agreeing with themselves, reinforcing fondly held prejudices.

Beware of these incestuous affinity groups. Sure, they make life less threatening. But they also make it terrible boring and predictable and repetitious. But the worst thing about getting stuck into some tight little circle—it doesn't encourage you to be you; it doesn't allow you to be you—to gain a sense of your own unique uniqueness. The ability to communicate, to express *your self*, requires you to know your self; to be your self.

FEAR OF FLYING

Stop the world, I want to get off

The flight crew that's been piloting Spaceship Earth through the 1960s, 70s, 80s and 90s will be relieved of their command in the new millennium when a brand-new crew takes over—you! That old crew will be turning over a planet that's been over-revved, under-maintained and loaded with enough explosives to blow us back to the Stone Age. So the new pilots better be made of the 'right stuff' to get everything back in working order.

Trouble is, many of you who should be attending flight school right now are A.W.O.L. So it's going to be a small graduating class that possesses the technical skills and mental toughness to handle the challenge. What's more, there are others who are fit for command but don't want the duty, preferring to go along for a free ride as passengers (in First Class, of course!). Then as soon as the ride gets a little bumpy, they will be the first to grab a parachute, press the panic button and look for the nearest exit.

If our planetary vehicle is going to make it through the 21st Century in one piece, everyone on board will have to contribute. If you elect to bail out, where will you land after the world has passed you by?

TEENAGE RIGHTS

N ot only do teenagers have legal rights—you have your very own Youth Law Center.

According to one such resource, nearly half the states in the U.S. have so-called "Child Emancipation" laws that permit a court to declare a child is grown-up before he or she reaches 18. This law requires the court, when petitioned by a minor, to determine if 1) the child can manage his/her finances, 2) whether emancipation is in the child's best interests, and 3) whether the parents agree to emancipation. (If the parents do not, emancipation becomes more complicated.)

Dependent minors who run afoul of the law and end up in reform school or juvenile detention center also have certain rights requiring separation from violent and adult detainees. You have a right to certain health services, access to family, friends and legal aid. Your rights also cover proper exercise and recreation, food, heat, light, clothing and a place to sleep. Nor can you be restrained by the use of handcuffs, shackles and isolation except in the most unusual circumstances. Your rights include protection from assault by other inmates.

Also, you have rights when it comes to school discipline. As the level of punishment increases, so do your rights. More details can be obtained from your community's Legal Aid society.

INTUITION: WHAT IT IS AND ISN'T AND WHY YOU CAN DEPEND ON THE REAL THING

The dictionary defines 'intuition' as knowing with out being able to trace the source of the knowing. But, recent research indicates intuition does indeed have a source. It turns out to be a facet of the nervous system.

It's an 'it,' so maybe now you'll trust it.

It really makes no difference to us non-scientists how intuition works. What matters is that it works! And yet we all have heard of cases where intuitive 'voices' prompted someone to go off half-cocked; sometimes to the extreme of killing. But such 'voices' were not intuition speaking. Impulses push you into wrong action. An impulse tends to be wishful thinking, a kind of hallucination.

No one can tell if the voice you hear is an echo of your desires or your intuition (only one of which should be listened to). If your past is pebbled with problems, chances are you should ignore the voice that whispers sweet nothings in your ear. But if everything is working out for you—trust it.

The voice of intuition doesn't rationalize; doesn't weigh the pluses and minuses. Your intuitive voice is confident, certain—it doesn't mince words. It comes from deep-down inside. It is the sound of you.

THE 'BEGINNER'S MIND'

The 'beginner's mind' is a phrase employed in Eastern philosophy meaning total receptivity to what is happening in one's own sphere. That's one (of the few) advantages a teenager has over adults. Experience tends to program people, set up preconceived notions about the way something is supposed to turn out rather than letting it unfold—i.e., being open to any possibility.

When you are past thirty or forty it is difficult to keep an open mind, but not impossible. So-called 'creative' people welcome the unexpected; do not feel threatened by the unknown. That's why artists and writers have a childlike quality about them, They are still full of the ol' Gee Whiz.

HARMONY

The highest and best use of this life experience surely is to live in harmony with our fellows and environment. That is, in fact, the very meaning of cosmos: a universe in harmony.

The basic stuff of the universe—atoms—is a study in harmony, as is that granddaddy of all atoms, the galaxies.

Someone who has been illumined by cosmic consciousness has had the transcending experience of feeling/being an intregal part of the whole (universe).

All kinds of good flows from 'living in harmony:' peace, freedom, good health, the ability to enjoy others. People with this quality are nice to be around, so they have lots of friends and lots of opportunity.

Living in harmony does not mean everyone marches to the same drummer. Harmony is a blending, an assembly of different notes that work together to create a pleasing effect. So harmony allows for the offbeat and the discordant.

All together now...

PATIENCE

High technology, especially television, has made us addicts for instant gratification. On TV we see lifetimes compressed into thirty-minute segments. Jets flash us across a continent, a trip that required three months of unimaginable hardship for our great-grandparents. So we have come to expect everything to happen (SNAP!) like that. And if it doesn't... forget it; life's too short.

This is an unfortunate development. It means too many people will never learn to play the piano, never climb Kilimanjaro or become neurosurgeons. Personal accomplishment still takes as long as ever. Skills are not learned in a day. Talent is not developed overnight.

Another reason for our impatience is that we have so much to choose from. It used to be that if you father was a stonemason, you'd be a stonemason—there was no choice. Coal miners' sons became coal miners and the offspring of gentry were destined to be gentry. Whereas today, we have a 'misery of choice.' A mason's son can grow up to be a labor leader. A shopkeeper's offspring can become a rock star. The mighty can fall and the fallen can rise. Because we can be just about anything we want, we tend to back away from something that requires perseverance, thinking that if one thing doesn't work out there'll be something else around the next corner.

Teenagers are inclined to be more impatient than your elders for the simple reason your past is so short; all your life experiences have happened in a relatively short time—your memories are hardly more than 10 years long. So committing your self to something that will require 5 years or more to perfect seems like an horrendous undertaking. You are equally impatient when it comes to problems and disappointments. When some girl or guy rejects you, or the coach demotes you—it seems like the end of the world. And it doesn't help when some grown-up says, "In a year from now you won't care" because a whole year equals a big hunk of your life to-date. Nothing anyone can say will change your perspective, but be a little patient with those who try.

WHY THE BEST OF TIMES ARE
THE WORST OF TIMES

In the dingy Dark Ages, after the Roman Empire folded and before the Renaissance bloomed, life wasn't worth living for 99% of mankind. Yet people didn't go around bitching about "these terrible times." People didn't know or expect anything but what they got: hunger, disease, misery, hopelessness.

You think you've got it bad? You have no idea what 'bad' is; how bad 'bad' can get.

Today we expect such a lot. We expect to work little and earn much. We expect never to go hungry, never to be treated unjustly. We expect to be well educated and well housed. Not that everyone is. But everyone expects it—thanks to the movies, TV, jet travel, the Internet and satellite communications.

Our expectations also are the product of man's stunning progress from dumb brute to demigod. As Heaven On Earth becomes a conceivable reality, anything that is less than heavenly is 1) noticed, and 2) resented. So we become rightly upset when some tinhorn Generalissimo tortures a few of his disloyal subjects. But no such hue and cry would have been raised just fifty years ago.

John Lennon was right back in '67 when he sang, "…it's getting bettah, getting bettah all the time…" And the more we expect, the better it will get.

There are some who say we are trying to progress too fast; to redress too many grievances and inequalities too soon. Blacks, Chicanos, the elderly, Vietnam vets, American indians, gays, Palestinians, Bosnians, Hutus, transsexuals, immigrants, the homeless… everyone is shouting, pushing and shoving to get their due, and complaining bitterly when it is denied them. Their wails are heard by all, thanks to the competitive electronic media. So we get the impression that there is so very much—maybe more than ever—injustice and suffering around us; so many wrongs to be righted.

Yet the fact is—never has there been more effort to help the helpless, with all kinds of positive results to show for it. Indians are given back their land. Cubans are given a home. Southeast Asians find refuge in the West. Minorities are receiving a much better education. Women get better pay and more equal access. The light of world opinion makes it increasingly difficult to repress human rights. There is much left to be done, God knows. But it is happening—now more than ever; faster than ever. It's as if the great mass of humanity had been feeling its way for centuries through a pitch-black, seemingly endless tunnel. Every inch gained was an agony. Only some inner spark lighted any hope and pushed one foot ahead of the other. Now, suddenly, a point of light is seen shining up ahead. The end of the tunnel is in sight!

Do you think so much humanity so long starved of hope will be content to continue shuffling slowly towards freedom? Hell no! A roar goes up and everyone stampedes for the exit.

And those who have been in charge of man's groping progress now find their orders, threats and entreaties have little effect. They are ignored, derided and run-over. That's because they are no longer needed to lead the way. Now people can see where they want to be. They also see their old warders—the generals, presidents, industrialists, bankers, policemen, ministers—stand between them and their expectations. Trouble is, the Old Guard is operating with its back to the future. To them it appears that people have lost their minds, rushing ahead shouting "Gimme, gimme, gimme."

No doubt about it, the first taste of freedom is intoxicating and causes people to act badly. Prison breaks are not an orderly process. So you hear a lot of tsk-tsking about how outstretched hands turn to fists. Sure, minorities enjoy more civil rights than they did fifty years ago, but they want even more, a predictable reaction to success, and a sure sign things are getting bettah all the time.

WHAT IF...

We waste an unholy amount of time applying hindsight to current events that affect us negatively. When something turns out bad, our imaginations rush to undo the event with *"What Ifs...,"* restructuring the negative outcome to produce the possibility of a different result. If it's an automobile accident—we go back a couple of blocks before the crash and wish we had missed one or more stoplights... which would have meant missing the truck that we in fact hit. Or, "If only I turned left on 3rd Avenue as I usually do instead of going straight on Main Street." Yes, and had we stayed in bed another 10 minutes this morning, that truck would not have been there when we crossed the intersection.

There's no end to such musings. "What if we hadn't moved to California last year?" "What if Mom and Dad had never been married?" "What if the Earth settled in an orbit a couple of million miles closer to the sun?"

Once an occurance occurs, it could not have occured any other way, with any other result. What is, *is*. What isn't, *isn't*. There is only one reality—i.e., there are no "might have beens", no other possibilities possible. The "What ifs..." only make you feel worse. We might better consider how it might have been worse. Included in those infinite *"What ifs..."*

are innumerable possiblities that might have killed or maimed you—e.g., if you had of reached that intersection one minute earlier, you would have collided with a speeding Fire Engine! How many times have you missed being mugged, hit by a falling safe, been aboard an aircraft that exploded in mid-air?? Count your blessings.

TIME HAPPENS

Time didn't start ticking the minute you were born. It just seems so.

Everything's new when you're new: every sight, sound, experience, realization is the first.

Your first kiss, as far as you're concerned, is the very first kiss ever kissed!

You discover a new word and presume it's new to everyone else. Indeed, with each new discovery, the discoverer is wont to stake a claim to it. But before you go running out into the street shouting, "Eureka! I have found it", remember—what's new to you is old to most of the rest of the world. Whatever you have imagined, conceived or thought of has undoubtedly been imagined, conceived and thought of many times before you.

This is not said to put down your discoveries. Far from it. You should be thrilled and delighted with each new encounter made along life's path—while knowing several billion minds have been busy before yours began its quest. And, who knows—your version may well be an improvement over the old.

And there always is the possibility that you may come up with something entirely new. Time will tell. (Lacking some sports-oriented 'first,' a scientific or patentable breakthrough, you might try manufacturing one out of whole cloth. For example, you could be first to fly a purple kite with a green tail over the Pentagon on a Sunday morning while entoning, "Thou Shalt Not Kill" one-thousand times. Or, you could try being the first 16-year old resident of Vermont to go 213 days without watching TV. Either one should qualify for the Guiness Book of Records.

FATTY FATTY TWO-BY-FOUR, CAN'T GET THROUGH THE SCHOOL ROOM DOOR

American teenagers not only are growing taller, you're growing *wider!* More precisely, you are getting fat. And flabby. (Could this be the reason you favor those baggy pants and sloppy sweat shirts?)

You don't have to look far to find the reasons so many terenagers are overweight.

You spend most of every day sitting. When you're not in the classroom, you're in front of a TV or computer screen, or sitting around some mall or wherever kids hang out where you live.

And only a third of you take Physical Ed classes on a daily basis. (At last count 15% of the U.S. states had no requirement for Physical Ed.) When school districts have to reduce their expenses, which is frequently, they do it at the expense of the Physical Ed Department.

Most of the overweight, under-active kids belong to parents who never work-out. It follows that millions of flabby kids are going to raise many more than that number of even flabbier kids. Like father, like son.

Kids who have no fitness role model to follow, seldom show any desire to stay fit. If you attend a school with no regular Physical Ed requirement, you're going to loose two ways: One you are likely to look ungainly and loose self-esteem. Two, kids who don't participate in organized group Physical Ed activities receive, as a group, lower grades while having the most discipline problems... and a negative self-image.

Then there is the matter of diet: Twinkies, fries and Big-Macs do not a healthy body make!

Maybe you don't care about your appearance (but, of course, you do!). And maybe you don't want to make a million dollars a day as a professional athlete (but, of course, you do!). But if you'd like to live long enough to get your money back from Social Security, you'd better watch your waist line. Because an fat teenager almost always grows into a fatter adult.

DROP-OUTS LOSE OUT

A University of California study has found that dropouts are twice as likely to lose their jobs than high-school graduates, and four times more likely than college grads. It also reports that each additional year of secondary school reduces the chance of being on welfare by 35%. And further, nearly 60% of all jail inmates did not complete high-school. What's more, earning a high-school diploma reduces your chances of being arrested by 90%.

It's too late for those tens of millions who have already dropped-out in the last decade. But it's not too late for you. Think long and hard before you follow their footsteps. Dropping-out is <u>not</u> the easy way out.

Another report on the same subject paints an equally black picture for dropouts. *Only 14% of new jobs in the U.S. can be filled by people with less than a high-school education.* And most of those jobs are menial, manual employment that lead nowhere and pay very little. This report goes on to say 52% of the new jobs that will be available between now at the year 2000 will require some college, while only 38% of the future workforce are in fact attending college. Obviously, the United States is facing a severe shortage of educated workers; a lack that will crimp the competitive status of American business and industry. Because most other industrialized countries have no shortage of well-educated workers, they will take up the slack caused by our social and educational system.

The real dummy here is the United States of America. This country should go back to school to study Socio-Economics 1A. That teaches it's far more cost-effective to properly educate the economically-deprived than it is to shut down factories and build bigger jails. There's no profit in punishment.

BETTER SADD THAN SORRY

Fifty years ago, teenagers lost friends to things like diphtheria, tuberculosis, poliomyelitis, and 101 other diseases—all of which immunization has elminated. Today, it's guns, alcohol, tobacco and drugs, mixed with 3,000 lbs. of speeding steel that kills young people.

No town, neighborhood or school is immune to this tragedy. There's no innoculation that that will make a drunk driver a safe driver. The only preventative medicine is called abstinence. When that fails, the only remedy is to prevent the drinker from driving. By persuasion if possible. If that doesn't move the driver out of harm's way, then remove your self as a passenger. A lousy way to end an evening. But consider the alternative!

Many times the driver won't give up the wheel and the passengers won't get out because it's a long, cold walk home. Asked why they didn't call their folks for help, most teenagers roll their eyes and shrug their shoulders—by way of saying, "Are you kidding? I'd rather take my chances on the road." Obviously you think your parents won't take kindly to being awakened in the wee hours for chauffeur duty. Nor are your parents overjoyed to hear you're with a bunch of drunks.

An organization exists to eliminate that "reason" for driving and drinking. S.A.A.D. (Students Against

Drunk Driving) has developed a "Contract For Life" for parents and teenagers. You agree not to drink and drive or be driven by anyone who has—calling your parents for a ride home, whatever the hour, however far. Your parents agree not to blame or punish or even bitch if you call for assistance.

This contract has served to remove many a zonked-out driver from behind the wheel. And when the driver won't cooperate, you can remove yourself from his car without having to make the long walk home. For some copies of their contract, write S.A.A.D., 110 Pleasant Street, Corbin Plaza, Marlboro, MA 01752, or for faster action call (617) 481-3568. If your school hasn't introduced the Student Body to this SAAD program, make it your Crusade to do so.

ADOLESCENT STRESS

Before getting into the subject at hand, a word about the word 'adolescent.' No self-respecting teenager likes to be called that. It sounds so... childish, not a lot better than 'kid.' Unfortunately, it is the proper word (albeit not a good-sounding word) for the teens. So please forgive its use here and elsewhere; it's not a put-down; it's just... a word.

Okay—now, about adolescent stress:

As covered in Chapter 1, this period of your life is highly stressful. Physical, social and psychological changes occur simultaneously, wham-bam! one on top of the other. Many teenagers respond to this onslaught by withdrawing—either slumping into passivity or becoming difficult and rebellious.

When adults—parents teachers and other authority figures— try to help, the over-stressed teenager is apt to react in a way that causes the adult to get angry, frustrated and, yes, intolerant. And that, of course, is what you were hoping for—it's your way of overcoming that helpless feeling. "Look! I'm able to drive my parents up the wall."

Most times, adolescent stress is manifested by slamming a door, turning up the decibels, mumbling, studying your shoe laces (if you have any), or whatever else you do to register your disapproval. You don't have a clue why you're acting this way. Parents, teachers, et al. should know why, but 'understanding' takes time, and that's what they have little of these days.

Of course what is considered 'maladjusted' behavior in one time and place, isn't in another. And the cure for it varies accordingly. Around here, today, your behavior may produce a pharmaceutical prescription or land you on some shrink's couch. Yet if you were born into a family of Laplanders, one night spent alone on the tundra would shape you up. Likewise, there was never a case of adolescent stress recorded during the great Irish famine, or if there was, no one noticed. "Stress" is a luxury to be enjoyed in relatively affluent times and places.

This is not to treat teenage ills lightly. Suicides among your age group have tripled in this past decade. And most of those happen in the affluent suburbs, not in the (hopeless) ghettos. Shocking as it is puzzling. It's not that today's teens are carrying around a lot more guilt. Punks don't feel guilty about being punks. The problems is more likely a lack of meaning in your lives—a 'who cares' or 'why care' attitude that had its beginning back when your parents were teenagers.

It is hoped the preceding chapters will encourage you to *press on, regardless*, to turn that corner and find a worthwhile future in front of you.

When you get down in the dumps, convinced there's nothing to live for, picture your self in some place like North Korea living on bark and roots. Or being forced to dig your own grave in Bosnia. A little transference goes a long way to putting your troubles into perspective. If you don't know or don't care how the rest of the world lives, another way to snap out of your doldrums and revive your enthusiasm is to exercise. When you least feel like it is when you most need it. Exercise pumps you up, gets you breathing deep, feeds oxygen into the bloodstream. Going full-tilt leaves you with little energy to think your self into knots.

Finally, you should be reminded what was mentioned in an earlier chapter: One reason your troubles/complaints/disappointments are so heavy is because they're so new. After all, you haven't spent the last ten years wrestling them. The first time a big disappointment hits, it hits hardest, hurts the worst. And when you only have one or two versus twenty problems to contend with, those one or two get blown up out of all proportion. You probably don't want to hear that—teens have a tendency to idolize and protect their problems, and to resent any effort to minimize them. But the title of this book obliges its author to make the effort. So don't say you weren't told.

THRILLAHOLICS

Psychologists have discovered that some people need thrills as diabetics need insulin. These congenital thrill-seekers are not necessarily braver or more courageous than we who are fearful of high-risk diversions. The reason they love high speed, falling out of airplanes, hanging upside down in amusement parks and other forms of torment is a neurological need for the bio-chemical state that is produced by intense excitement. They have an imbalance of a brain chemical called *monoamine oxidaze,* which causes depression. Risk/fear seems to change the levels of that chemical, lifting them from torpor to elation. In other words, *being scared to death makes them feel alive!*

So don't think you're a fraidycat to avoid Horror Movies, rollercoasters or steep mountainsides covered with slippery snow. You don't need a shot of *monoamine oxidaze.* They do.

GIVE & GET

People who always give of themselves and their property don't do it because it hurts. Quite the contrary. It makes them feel good! They receive an immediate pay back, an injection of self-esteem, among other things.

Young people have spent most of their years receiving. You receive food, shelter, clothing, medical care, love. (Some of you receive more; some less.) Society gives you an education, roads, sewers, protection... without asking anything in return, except perhaps obedience.

Lately, there's a movement afoot to give you an opportunity to give—in order to receive the glow produced by selfless service to others. Like so many new ideas, this one was first planted in California by a State Legislature Panel on Self-Esteem. This august panel has created the Human Corps Task Forces on all the state's four-year public campuses. College students are asked to perform community service an average of 30 hours a year. This produced the Community Involvement Center at San Francisco State University, Y.E.S. at Humbolt State, and similar groups at UC Berkeley and at Stanford. What about your campus? High school? How about installing something similar?

Of course you always can give of yourself individually. Wherever you live, you're surrounded with people who need help—especially elderly people. Just being around young people makes their old bones feel better. The phone book is full of places who care for the elderly. They are always under-staffed and would welcome your helping hands.

Anytime is a goodtime to give time. But the very best time is when you yourself are having a bad time. When you spend time helping others, there's no time to feel sorry for yourself.

THE GLOBAL VILLAGE

This book is not addressed to San Francisco kids, or California kids, or American kids. In this day and age young people belong to a larger community, the "Global Village"... a village created by TV, the world wide web, telecommunications and supersonic travel. The realization of this may be sometime catching up to the reality—but the generation that follows you will consider teenagers in the Balkans (you do know where the Balkans are, don't you?) as much a part of their scene as kids from the next town are now.

This enlarged sense of community will help wipe out borders and other arbitrary differences that promote differences/intolerance/wars/ad naseam. It will also give rise to a Collective Consciousness that is a zillion times more powerful than the sum total of individuals it comprises. That is the basis of Esprit d'Corps; team spirit... what it takes to do better than your best. An eleven man football squad suddenly jells into a harmonious team, rising to a level that was quite beyond the eleven individuals involved. This is synergy; what it takes to overcome great odds and accomplish great feats. This force works for both good and evil. It worked for Nazi stormtroopers; it worked for George Washington's beleaguered revolutionaries; it's how underdogs become topdogs. It overcame discrimination in the American South, and it will usher in the new Era of Interdependence. May The Force be with you always.

VISITING HOURS WITH YOUR SELF

Choosing to be alone with your self is a choice you may not be able to make in the years ahead. The world is becoming too crowded to make solitude convenient.

Except for the few minutes a day we spend in the toilet/bathroom, we are always surrounded with others by choice or not. No wonder young people do not know the value of aloneness and why we connect it with loneliness.

Not only is solitude inconvenient; we do not miss it, much less seek it. Indeed, we actively avoid it, as if it were a form of punishment —i.e., solitary confinement.

All our training emphasizes interpersonal relationships—how to get along with others. Because there are so many 'others' to get along with, this is a desirable skill. But how about getting along with our selves? If we do not feel comfortable with our selves; how in hell are we to get along with others?

There is a program called Vision Quest that takes young people into wilderness areas (after appropriate preparation and other safeguards) where they are left alone separated by at least a mile for two days and two nights to face the environment and them selves. Fasting during the 48-hour vigil is an important part of the ritual as it tends to cleanse the body and purify the mind so that unalloyed vision may be experienced.

This is a modern-day version of the American Indian Rites Of Passage whereby the future brave returned to his tribe more confident of his manhood.

Teens (of both sexes) return to there base camp centered as never before, having faced their selves for the first time. They don't come back new persons necessarily, but they come back with a better sense of 'self' (sometimes called 'self-identity')) which translates to self-confidence and self-esteem.

Unfortunately few of you will have the opportunity to participate in an organized Vision Quest. But at the very least, do not avoid opportunities to be alone with your self... whether on a hilltop or a park bench. Friends are important; friends are great. But it also is beneficial to shut off the 'buzz' of society and seek solitude if only for a few hours. It may not prove enjoyable; it may even be unnerving. In that case, it is much needed. Try it. ASAP.

HOW TO MOVE MOUNTAINS
(WHEN YOU'RE 18)

The world we live in is composed of mountains of greed; mountains of indifference; mountains of prejudice and inhuman treatment... all of which can be removed with a single vote. Not just anyone's vote, but *your* vote.

You've heard it said, many times, that *every vote counts*. But when you consider the number of votes involved in a national election—tens of millions— your one vote seems so immaterial, so unimportant... especially when the other party or candidate is favored by millions. Yet look what happens when you and a lot of other voters don't register and/or don't register their preference on election day. You allow a minority to rule the majority. Historically, the people with the most to gain, the needy (the 'have-nots'), stay home allowing the greedy (the 'haves') to prevail. But an even worse voting record belongs to the people who have the most to lose—young (18 to 25) voters. Your silence has proved the undoing of candidates and issues who stood for the common good...*your* good! You have to live with the consequences for the next half century. By not voting you assured the continued deterioration of the environment; the continued outpouring of wealth and resources into unneeded armaments at the expense of human needs. It is a sad and sorry testimony that every four years young people have an opportunity to move that mountain we call "The Military-Industrial Complex." But each time young voters are a "No Show"; instead of lifting their ballots, they lowered their heads and wandered off to become voices complaining in the wilderness of their own discontent. Maybe young people would benefit from a few score years spent under the iron heel of some jackbooted tyrant to properly appreciate the benefits and obligations of a representative government.

If those of you who reach voting age in time for the next election don't do better than your predecessors—you just may be able to sample the benevolence of a "democratic" dictatorship.

THOUGHT-RELEASE CAPSULES

on LOVE

What would youth be without love?

—Byron

True love doesn't bind; it frees.

—Unknown

Loving your self will dissolve your ego; you will feel no need to prove you are superior. And the more loving you are, the more loving are those around you: Play a happy tune and happy dancers will join you.

—*The Lazy Man's Guide to Enlightenment*

Peace can only be made by those who are peaceful, and love can only be shown by those who love.

—Alan Watts

If you learn to love, you will do all things well.

—Unknown

You can give without loving, but you can't love without giving.

—Unknown

on TRUST

He who does not trust enough will not be trusted.

—Lao-Tsu

Trust the Universe. Do not feel diminished by its immensity. The cosmos bears witness to your immensity, for you are it and it is you.

—Alan Watts

on MONEY

Money is a terrible master but an excellent servant.

—B.T. Barnum

Blessed are the young, for they shall inherit the national debt.

—Herbert Hoover

Young people nowadays imagine that money is everything, and when they grow older they know it.

—Oscar Wilde

Work is the price you pay for money.

—Anon.

on SUCCESS & FAILURE

I cannot give you a formula for success, but I can give you the formula for failure: try to please everybody.

—Herbert Bayard Swope

Success often comes from taking a misstep in the right direction.

—Anon.

The most important single ingredient in the formula of success is knowing how to get along with people.

—Theodore Roosevelt

Be awful nice to 'em goin' up, because you're gonna meet'em all comin' down.

—Jimmy Durante

Show me a good loser and I'll show you a loser.

—Jimmy Carter

Trying is another word for failing.

—Samm

The Lord gave us two ends—one to sit on and the other to think with. Success depends on which one we use the most.

—Ann Landers

on POSSESSIONS

... not collecting treasures prevents stealing. Not seeing desirable things prevents confusion of the heart.

—Unknown

Amass a store of gold and jade, and no one can protect it.

He who knows he has enough is rich.

—Lao-tsu

on HONESTY

Truth gets you high. Lies bring you down.

—Ram Dass

It is an honest man who admits to telling the occasional fib.

—Samm

on OPPOSITION

A certain amount of opposition is a great help. Kites rise against the wind and not with the wind.

—John Neal

All can see beauty as beauty only because there is ugliness. All can know good as good only because there is evil.

—Unknown

That which shrinks must first expand. That which fails must first be strong. That which is cast down must first be raised. Before receiving there must be giving. This is called perception of the nature of things.

—Lao-tsu

Opposites create a worthwhile tension. Any structure, whether physical in nature or institutional, will collapse without tension. Cultures and empires dissolve because of success (the absence of tension). It is opposition that creates balance and harmony. Without the 'Nays' to balance the 'Ayes,' equilibrium is lost; that is why tyrannies are short-lived.

—Samm

on *HOW TO BE MISERABLE*

1. Use 'I' as often as possible.
2. Always be sensitive to slights.
3. Be jealous and envious.
4. Trust no one.
5. Never forget a criticism
6. Always expect to be appreciated.
7. Look for faults in others.
8. Don't give until you get.

—Unknown

on *PARTICIPATING*

You can't play the game of life sitting on the sidelines.

—Samm

on *HEALTH*

Every second, 2,500,000 red blood cells in your body are being destroyed, and 2,500,000 more are being created. The breakdown of old forms is needed for health. When you don't exercise, you don't break down enough red cells and some of the worn-out ones stay around. Then you wonder why you don't feel so good.

—George Leonard

on CIVICS

... leading yet not dominating, this is the Primal Virtue.

Why are the people rebellious? Because the rulers interfere too much.

Force is followed by a loss of strength.

The more laws and restrictions there are, the poorer
    people become;
the sharper men's weapons, the more trouble in the
    land;
the more ingenious and clever men are, the more
    stranger things happen;
the more rules and regulations, the more thieves and
    robbers.

—Lao-tsu

Laws are like cobwebs, which may catch small flies but let wasps and hornets break through.

—Jonathan Swift

on VIOLENCE & ANGER

Anger is just one letter short of 'danger.'

—Della Reese

Violence, whether or a mass scale or between individuals, happens when fear or anger interferes with communication. When you are angry or fearful, your breath comes short; it's difficult to speak or to speak sensibly because you have lost *self*-control. In frustration, you strike out.

The parent who punishes a child with physical force, or threatens to, is 'saying' he/she has lost the ability to communicate—which is to lose one's humanity.

—Samm

on QUIETUDE

Those who know do not talk.
The quieter you become, the more you hear.

—Unknown

Just be here now.

—Ram Dass

on YOUTH

In his youth, everybody believes that the world began to exist only when he was born, and that everything really exists for his sake.

—Goethe

Youth is wasted on the young.

—G.B. Shaw

Young men, in the conduct and manage of actions, embrace more than they can hold; stir more than they can quiet; fly to the end without consideration of the means...

—Francis Bacon

Every generation is a secret society and has incommunicable enthusiasms, tastes, and interests which are a mystery both to its predecessors and to posterity.

—Chapman

Youth is America's oldest tradition.

—Oscar Wilde

on YOUTH & AGE

Every old man complains of the growing depravity of the world, of the petulance and insolence of the rising generation.

The conversation of the old and the young ends generally with contempt on either side.

—Samuel Johnson

If youth but knew; if old age could!

—Henri Estienne

The excesses of our youth are drafts upon our old age, payable with interest about thirty years after date.

—C.C. Coleridge

One thing only has been lent to youth and age in common—discontent.

—Mathew Arnold

on FREEDOM

If you are to get out of prison, the first thing you must realize is: you are in prison! If you think you are free, you can't escape.

—Gurdjieff

on EVERYTHING

Where it's at is seldom where it seems to be.

Smoothing rough spots sometimes requires abrasives.

There are no exceptions to the rule that everyone likes to be an exception to the rule.

243

Experts are those whose opinions agree with my own.

Misfortune comes from having a body. Without a body and its partner, the ego, how could there be misfortune?

Forever is a longtime, but not as long as it was yesterday.

Stay conscious of your consciousness.

He who searches for God has found him.

Life is celebration.

—Unknown

By the time a man realizes that maybe his father was right, he usually has a son who thinks he's wrong.

—Charles Wadsworth

He who hesitates is last.

—Mae West

Act the way you'd like to be and soon you'll be the way you act.

—Dr G.W. Crane

Go as far as you can see and when you get there you'll see further...

—L. Ron Hubbard

There is nothing good now bad that thinking does not make.

Words without thoughts never to Heaven go.

—Shakespeare

Training is everything. The peach was once a bitter almond; cauliflower is nothing but cabbage with a college education.

—Mark Twain

Happiness is accepting what-is.

—Werner Erhard

It is only when you are pursued that you become swift.

—Kahlif Gibran

The present is the only thing without end.

Purpose? What purpose does a Universe of a billion galaxies serve?

No one can hinder or hurt you; aid or assist you without your agreement.

The same soil nurtures all plant life, from the lowly weed to the mighty sequoia.

People who like many things are most likable.

Our opinions of others too often are expressed in terms of what we don't like about them. This makes our ego think better of itself. That's how the ego grows—by comparing.

—Samm

in CONCLUSION

YOU CAN NO LONGER DECEIVE YOURSELVES
AS YOU DID BEFORE.
YOU NOW HAVE GOT THE TASTE OF TRUTH.
—Ouspensky

AFTERWORD

*Wherein the constant reader is congratulated
and The Millennium previewed*

Now that The End is here, the author is going to break the rule that's eliminated his
"I" person from all the preceding pages.
That's because I wish to congratulate you. And well
you deserve to be saluted.

Look what a lot of territory you've covered: 249
pages jampacked with new thoughts, wild ideas, pro-
vocative precepts, controversial concepts... about
emotionally-charged subjects like how-to-save-the
world without-even-trying, highs & lows, life & death,
Heaven & Hell, S-E-X, parents, school, drugs, what
makes you tick—none of it written in teenage jargon
(which changes too fast to publish!).

If you can relate to even half of what's been laid
down, you deserve an "A."

You're not expected to do anything in particular with what you've read, or even agree with any of it. The purpose of these pages is to put points of view on display—ways to cope and survive; to grow and thrive. If you choose to reject this or that—fine. Terrific! Because you can't very well shoot down an idea without considering it—letting it into your consciousness. And every time your consciousness opens to let in something new, it expands, becomes more flexible, more aware. That's what the world needs—more awareness; more open minds.

"Teenagers won't read that stuff," I was warned. "You're wasting your time."

"They read their own mail, don't they?" I replied, and continued writing.

The answer to that is the tens of thousands of copies that have found their way to teenagers via schools, grand parents, local libraries, churches, detention centers, an anxious auntie and word of mouth.

There's more to it than that. There's more going on behind your eyes than meets the eye. Your interest and perception offers hope for the future ... for this country, this race, this planet and the cosmos containing all of the above.

Of course, a couple of hundred thousand perceptive readers is not exactly the whole world. Ah, but it is enough to change the world. A handful of enlightened young people are a force to be reckoned with! There are plenty of examples of a small cadre changing the course of human history, for better or for worse. Jesus and a few disciples changed the world for the better. Whereas a guy named Hitler with his gaggle of crazed cronies gave the world two black eyes.

Which gets me to the point of this whole publishing effort: To help actualize a breakthrough—whereby mankind takes a quantum leap forward to a higher level of consciousness en route to the ultimate objective, *Heaven On Earth*, a state of grace that is only possible when everyone treats everyone else as they would be treated themselves.

That will happen sooner or later (if mankind doesn't trip over its technology in the meantime), whether or not anyone reads these paragraphs. But on the chance a few well-chosen words can hasten that day; they should be writ!

Homo sapiens has made such leaps before. Going from the Dark Ages into the Renaissance was one. It had a trigger. As will the upcoming breakthrough.

Possibly, just maybe, your generation will be the one to write history instead of repeating, repeating, repeating it. All it takes is an enlightened elite… leadership that inspires without dominating. Might not the readers of these pages be such avatars, lighting the way to that higher level of conscious awareness? You have all the necessary qualifications.

When it does happen, there will be no missing it. Such breakthroughs are not slow, gradual transitions.

They are bounding leaps, cosmic bridges leading from darkness to radiance—not inch by inch but in a sudden burst of energy; a spiritual blossoming that can turn cannons into ploughshares. It will lead to a moral rearmament—a society of equals dedicated to the upgrading of the human mind, body and spirit. It can and will happen in one generation, if not today, some day. When it does, it will be no miracle but what happens when an accumulation of all the right thoughts and actions becomes so dense, it explodes with a force greater than the sum of its parts. The fallout will shower "Cosmic Consciousness" on us all, illuminating the dark corners of the past.

Some might relate this to "The Second Coming." Whatever it is, that Great Day will dawn the moment self-esteem gains dominion over no-esteem ... when there are more people who basically like themselves than there are who wish to hide from themselves.

That greatday is a-comin'. Anything you can do to help hasten it will be very much appreciated. (What exactly you have to "do," or be, I'm sure I don't know; probably nothing more than to remain aware of that goal. That should do it.)

In any case, it's your world. Make the most of it.

ABOUT
THE
AUTHOR

Mr. Coombs was an advertising copywriter to start with. After going about as far as one can go in the ad world—at 39 he was President of a major west coast advertising agency—Samm became an agent of change, launching the country's first public interest ad agency to help good causes deliver their message. He co-founded a self-realization center for young adults—an experience that led to writing this book. Mr. Coombs makes no claim to being a professional in the field of juvenile behavior. "My certification comes from the School of Hardknocks, having been a teenager and raising three of my own."

The author's literary credits cover a wide variety of subjects, including dangerous avocations (*Edgework*), the environment (*Green Christmas*), baseball ((*America's National Game*), and the California gold rush (*Wining,*

Dining & Reclining With The 49ers). Mr. Coombs' latest book, *TIME HAPPENS,* treats the flipside of adolescence: the frantic fifties.

When he isn't writing books and articles, Samm may be founded speaking to youth groups, parenting organizations and senior councils, or rollerblading to the nearest tennis court playing the harmonica en route.

Mr. Coombs was born, raised and educated in the San Francisco Bay Area where he presently resides.

(RE)ORDERING TEENAGE SURVIVAL MANUAL

Retail booksellers should order from their wholesaler or from Halo's distributor, APG Trade, 3356 Coffey Lane, Santa Rosa, CA 95403. 800-327-5113 East of the Rockies; 800-275-2606 West of the Rockies.

Readers, whether for yourself or others, may order direct from the publisher in the event the book is not found in your local book stores. See order form opposite.

Churches, non-profit organizations, public service agencies, schools/teachers, librarians and other professionals may qualify for quantity discounts. For information write Halo at the address opposite or call 415/981-5144; 892-0649.

Groups, clubs and organizations who may wish to use the book as a premium or for fund-raising should contact publisher.

Price/discounts subject to change without notice.

ORDER FORM

To: Halo Books, LLC
    P.O. Box 2529
    San Francisco, CA 94126

I enclose check/money order payable to Halo Books in the amount of $_____ for books noted on list below. (Add $2.50 for shipping one book and $1.75 for each additional book. California residents please include 7% sales tax.

Mail to:
Name_____
Street address_____
Town _____State____ZIP_____
Please send:

___copies of TEENAGE SURVIVAL MANUAL,
        Being in charge of your
        own mind and body
            Coombs $14.95 ea

___copies of TIME HAPPENS,
        You could not have picked
        a better time to be fiftysomething
            Coombs $13.95 ea

___copies of A GARDEN OF WOMAN'S
WISDOM, *A Secret Haven for Renewal*
Veltri $12.95 ea

___copies of SUDDENLY SINGLE,
A Lifeline for Anyone
Who Has Lost a Love
Larson $13.95 ea

___copies of THIS ISN'T EXACTLY WHAT I
HAD IN MIND, GOD,
How to get your life back on track
Larson $14.95 ea.

___copies of IF HE LOVES ME, WHY DOESN'T
HE TELL ME?
Larson $12.95 ea

___copies of AM I A HINDU?
The Hinduism primer
Viswanathan $15.95 ea

___copies of YOUR SEXUAL HEALTH
What teenagers need to know about sexually-
transmitted diseases and pregnancy
McClosky $15.95 ea

For a free catalog of all Halo Books in print,
write address above. Thank you.